From Teacher to
Middle Manager

_____

LEADERSHIP SKILLS IN EDUCATION MANAGEMENT SERIES

Series Editor: Professor Trevor Kerry

Other titles in this series

Mastering Deputy Headship   **Professor Trevor Kerry**
This practical book sets out to not only identify but address the issues facing newly appointed deputies and also those who are aspiring to become a deputy head. It aims to examine the generic skills needed within such a role.

The Special Educational Needs Coordinator   **Vic Shuttleworth**
This practical book enables aspiring or newly appointed SENCOs (Special Educational Needs Coordinators) to approach a range of management tasks with the right knowledge and techniques to work systematically and effectively with colleagues, benefiting the most vulnerable pupils and cutting through the layers of bureaucracy to expose the bigger issues.

Head Teacher in the 21st Century   **Frank Green**
Head Teacher in the 21st Century looks at providing a strategy for aspiring or actual postholders which can be used to systematically monitor and improve their own performance. Using case studies and practical tasks, it examines how to develop the skills needed to be an effective head teacher and leader.

For further information,
telephone Pearson Education Ltd
on 01279 623333.

From Teacher to
Middle Manager

Making the next step

Susan Tranter

Pearson
Education

PEARSON EDUCATION LIMITED

Head Office:
Edinburgh Gate
Harlow CM20 2JE
Tel: +44 (0)1279 623623
Fax: +44 (0)1279 431059

London Office:
128 Long Acre
London WC2E 9AN
Tel: +44 (0)20 7447 2000
Fax: +44 (0)20 7240 5771
Website: www.business-minds.com

First published in Great Britain in 2000

© Pearson Education Limited 2000

The right of Susan Tranter to be identified as Author
of this Work has been asserted by her in accordance
with the Copyright, Designs and Patents Act 1988.

ISBN 0 273 65097 1

British Library Cataloguing in Publication Data
A CIP catalogue record for this book can be obtained from the British Library.

10 9 8 7 6 5 4 3

Typeset by Boyd Elliott Typesetting
Printed and bound in Great Britain by Bell & Bain Ltd., Glasgow

The Publishers' policy is to use paper manufactured from sustainable forests.

Contents

About the author   viii
Series editor's introduction   ix
List of tasks   xi
List of tables   xii
List of figures   xiv
Preface   xv
How to use this book   xvi

1   Acquiring skills and experiences   1
    Developing excellence   2
    Differentiation   12
    Leading and managing projects   17
    Delegation   19
    Being a life-long learner   20
    Starting to look for a post   22
    Summary   25

2   Making the application and preparing for interview   27
    Core purposes   28
    Professionalism   32
    Motivation   37
    Information sources   41
    Planning an application   43
    Summary   63

3   Starting out   65
    Appointments   66
    Visiting the new school   68
    Getting to know everyone   75

Setting the agenda for the first few months   86
Taking care of yourself   86
Leading change   88
Time management   98
Summary   102

4   Developing a vision   103
What are leadership and management?   104
Power and authority   109
Management models   113
Developing a vision   115
Communicating the vision   117
Constructing a development plan   127
Making sure the development plan is carried out   133
Summary   134

5   Links with senior staff and peers   137
Line management   139
Being managed   148
Appraisal   149
Administrative control   163
Team reports   165
Summary   169
Appendix – an Annual Report   170

6   Recruiting and monitoring staff   181
Motivation   183
Preparing to recruit   187
Interview day   192
Conducting an interview   196
Recruiting a deputy subject leader   199
Managing the induction of new staff   201
Monitoring and evaluation   202
Summary   205

7   Making presentations   207
    Planning the content   208
    Deciding the form   211
    Making an impact   216
    Presentations to parents   218
    Summary   224

8   Professional development   225
    Management   226
    Organisational theory   227
    Teachers as learners   232
    Summary   234

    References   235
    Index   237

About the author

Susan Tranter has worked in a number of secondary schools. Her career began teaching Mathematics at a boys' school. Her responsibilities have included Head of Sixth Form, Head of Mathematics, Primary Liaison, Teaching and Learning. Her teaching career has been in inner-city schools and rural schools. She has postgraduate degrees in Pure Mathematics and Management in Education. More recently she was one of the first to complete the NPQH course. Susan is currently sole Deputy Headteacher of an Oxford comprehensive school.

Series editor's introduction

The nature of schools and the educative process is changing. Indications are that the first decade of the twenty-first century will see the fastest, and the most far-reaching, changes in schools and schooling since the compulsory education system was established. The signs are there if we have eyes to see them:

- advances in technology will alter the nature of learning. While school has been characterised by the need for groups of people to assemble together to listen to a teacher, the computer, its software and the Internet are making learning accessible to anyone, according to need and inclination, without their having to come together;

- technology, through the computer and through video-conferencing, gives access on a local level to global opportunities. If they have the technology, pupils in Britain can access the very best lessons and the very best teachers from anywhere in the world. In place of thousands of teachers teaching thousands of different, more or less good, lessons on a topic, the student will be able to access the most complete and dynamic lesson regardless of where it is taught;

- computers even threaten the concept of school time. Since the computer gives access at unlimited times and in unlimited places, learning need no longer be associated with time slots at all;

- but it is not just computers that are driving the forces of education into new channels. Economics plays a part. School buildings are inflexible and costly, yet they often remain unused for more than 80 per cent of the time – during vacations, evenings, nights and so on. Costly plant lying idle is a luxury that society may feel unable to afford;

- increasingly, we can see non-teachers of various kinds becoming more central to the education process. There was a time when no adult but a teacher would have been found in a classroom. Now schools often have a greater complement of technicians, administrators, nursery assistants, special needs assistants, students from care courses, voluntary helpers and counsellors than they do of teaching staff.

So key areas – how learning takes place, where it takes place, when, its quality, the type of plant required, the nature of the people who deliver it – are all in the melting pot as we enter the new millennium. If ever there was a moment for developing a new breed of educational leaders who could span the effective management of the present system and forge a path into the future, this is it.

This series is therefore dedicated to achieving those ends: to help education managers at various levels in the system to become the leaders now and the pioneers of the future. The titles are all written by people with proven track records of innovation. The style is intended to be direct, and the reader is asked to engage with the text in order to maximise the training benefit that the books can deliver.

Change is rarely comfortable, but it can be exciting. This series hopes to communicate to school leaders something of the confidence that is needed to manage change, and something of the fulfilment that comes from meeting challenge successfully.

Professor Trevor Kerry

List of tasks

1	Developing subject knowledge	3
2	Preparing to differentiate a topic	12
3	Selecting a strategy for differentiation	15
4	Analysing a job description	22
5	The meaning of the core purpose statement	29
6	Identifying the attributes and skills of the professional teacher	34
7	Identifying your motivation	37
8	Analysing information on a school	43
9	Responding to a person specification	50
10	Responding to a job description	51
11	Analysing a letter of application	55
12	Interview questions	61
13	Preparing for initial meetings 1	69
14	Preparing for initial meetings 2	72
15	Finding out about your team	76
16	Identifying cultural characteristics	88
17	Urgent v. important	98
18	Are you a good leader?	104
19	Constraints on progress	110
20	Identifying influences on your team's work	115
21	Communicating the vision to the team	118
22	Managing responses	122
23	Analytical and functional monitoring	142
24	Collecting information for performance appraisal	153
25	Linking performance targets to the school development plan	161
26	Reporting on the team's work	166
27	Personal motivation factors	185
28	Assessing candidates at interview	193
29	Defining the role of the deputy subject leader	199
30	Planning a presentation	209
31	Decision making	228
32	Decision making at your school	230

List of tables

1.1	Ofsted criteria for assessing the quality of teaching	9
1.2	Topic analysis: skills, outcomes, methods	13
1.3	Topic analysis: planning document model	14
1.4	Ten differentiation strategies	15
1.5	Input, process and outcome differentiation – benefits and consequences	16
1.6	Job description for a Head of Mathematics	23
2.1	Analysis of the core purpose of a subject leader	30
2.2	Attributes of some of the professions	32
2.3	Features of teachers in different educational phases	34
2.4	Motives for seeking promotion	37
2.5	Middle management posts: responsibilities and implications	38
2.6	School information analysis proforma	44
2.7	Information indicators	48
2.8	Person specification for Head of Modern Languages	50
2.9	A middle manager's job description	51
2.10	Points to remember when completing an application form	54
2.11	Application letter model	55
2.12	An example of a letter of application	56
2.13	A model CV	58
2.14	Selection day events with notes and comments	59
2.15	Interview questions	61
3.1	Actions on being appointed	67
3.2	The importance of preparing for initial meetings	69
3.3	Preparing for the first team meeting	72
3.4	Finding out about your team	77
3.5	Team profile proforma	80
3.6	Teacher observation feedback proforma	83
3.7	Cultural characteristics	89
3.8	Categories of middle manager-led strategic change	90
3.9	Model for strategic change	93

3.10	Planning change	94
3.11	Events in the day of the head of English	99
3.12	The head of English's response	100
4.1	Secrets of leadership	105
4.2	Bush's models of power and authority in schools	109
4.3	Aspects of children's development and their implications	111
4.4	Management models and the middle manager	113
4.5	Developing a sense of direction for your team's work	116
4.6	The team's needs	118
4.7	Team strengths and weaknesses	120
4.8	Implications of the vision	121
4.9	Predicting and managing the team responses	122
4.10	Improvement plan for a Mathematics department	128
4.11	Addressing targets through an improvement plan	133
5.1	Line management	139
5.2	Stages Joanne needs to follow	141
5.3	Teacher activities at Joanne's school	142
5.4	Characteristics of effective monitoring	148
5.5	Being line-managed	149
5.6	Gold and Szemerenyi's appraisal system objectives	150
5.7	Performance indicators and evidence	153
5.8	Data collection	154
5.9	Outcomes and targets	157
5.10	Summary of the appraisal process	159
5.11	Linking performance targets to the SDP (1)	161
5.12	Linking performance targets to the SDP (2)	162
5.13	Administrative control	164
5.14	The team report	165
5.15	A framework for the reporting of a team's work	166
6.1	Motivation factors	185
6.2	Team needs audit proforma	187
6.3	The usefulness of interview tasks	194
6.4	Interview questions	196
6.5	Summary of the recruitment process	198
6.6	Summary of the monitoring process	205
7.1	Tips for effective delivery of a presentation	217
7.2	Planning a parent information event	218
7.3	The practicalities of a parents' event	223
8.1	Decision making – Weber's model	228
8.2	Comparing organisational perspectives	231
8.3	Brighouse and Woods' seven processes	232
8.4	Gaining involvement in senior management tasks	233

List of figures

7.1   Mind-map of planning a presentation on underachieving boys   210

Preface

The readers of this book will be teachers at varying stages of their careers and in a wide-ranging variety of posts. For some they will be starting their career and be thinking about their progression to middle management and beyond. For others they will have been in teaching a while and planning their move into middle management. Some, it is hoped, will be existing middle managers who want new ideas and who are looking for a fresh challenge to this important role in the work of any school. These people will be found in all sectors of education – from colleges of education, to primary and secondary schools.

This book begins with assumption that every teacher wants to be the best teacher he/she can be. Some teachers are able to examine their own practice and move themselves forward. They have a clear idea of what is required and where they want to be next. For others, however, though there is a genuine desire to improve and progress they need guidance from those who have gone before. Teaching and management share the fact that they are both ever changing. They are both dynamic activities that directly impinge on the quality of people's personal and professional lives. The quality of teaching will affect the teacher's career because of the success he/she is able to bring about in his/her pupils. It will affect the teacher's professional success because to be an effective middle manager, excellence in teaching is a necessity.

The role of the middle manager in school has changed a good deal. Gone for ever is the person who ordered the books – although controlling resources and budget management is a chapter in this book. Less important now is the Head of Subject who is the most knowledgeable about the subject. More important now is the Head of Subject who is an excellent teacher. This Head of Subject's expertise lies in ensuring that the subject is delivered in a consistently high-quality way.

This is not to denigrate the importance of subject expertise. There is a need for well-qualified experts to take on these important roles. However, the middle manager is the 'first among equals'. Middle managers are responsible for the work of the team and this book seeks to address the elements that go to make successful and purposeful leadership of a team possible.

How to use this book

This book is about management and leadership of a team of people, i.e. being a middle manager. The book takes readers from their first stage in the teaching profession through to making the application for a middle management role. It moves on to consider styles of management and leadership and the practical elements to effective and successful practice. The book uses a variety of means to set out, examine and exemplify the skills and techniques:

- text – to provide information, discussion and advice
- tables and figures – in some cases these are management models that are best explained in this way
- lists – to provide readers with a checklist of important points/things to remember
- activities and case studies – to enable readers to think through the issues raised in the text and to consider practical solutions to real life problems
- summaries – set out the main points of ideas and theories considered.

This book can be used in a variety of ways. It was written in some respects as a progression through the job and can be seen as an agenda for the middle manager. Alternatively, the reader may wish to 'dip in' to various sections – perhaps in response to a difficulty or as a means to thinking through a pertinent issue. A group of teachers may wish to use this book as a training manual, working through the sections together and discussing the main points. This would be an excellent means of sharing ideas and good practice.

This book is meant to be a practical tool that enables readers to think through the issues and make their own decisions. It is based on the premise that management and leadership skills can be acquired and practised. Its rationale is that of principle-centred management. As such, although there is reference to theory and there is a bibliography at the end, it is a practical book written by a practitioner. Practice without theory is without the necessary foundations. Without a sound basis, it can so easily be the result of luck rather than considered action.

chapter one

Acquiring skills and experiences

Developing excellence

Differentiation

Leading and managing projects

Delegation

Being a life-long learner

Starting to look for a post

Summary

At the start of a career, some will be aiming for the top (whatever that is) and others will be thinking about how they are going to make their way through their first few years in the profession. For many, their career path is a blend of serendipity and opportunity. However, aspiring middle managers need to consider the skills and attributes they will need if they are to progress to the role.

The most important quality, in our view, that you need to develop is that of excellence in the classroom. It is essential if you are to have a successful career at middle and senior levels.

This chapter will discuss the following issues that are important when planning a career in teaching:

■ how to become an excellent teacher

■ how to take a long-term view on career planning

■ the first few years

■ planning a project

■ what issues to concentrate upon

■ leading a project and working with others

■ professional development courses – the importance of Masters degrees and the like and how to incorporate these into the schedule

■ the essential and desirable attributes for middle management.

_____ Developing excellence _____

One way of identifying the qualities displayed by a teacher described as excellent, is by referring to the Ofsted documents on this subject. Ofsted inspectors are required to report on the quality of teaching, judged in terms of its impact on learning and what makes it successful or not. There are a number of other features on which Ofsted inspectors must report and these include:

- how well the skills of literacy and numeracy are taught
- how well the teaching meets the needs of all the pupils and students
- how well pupils and students make progress.

These are judgements and evaluations based on the quality of teaching and learning – the central question is: "How well are pupils or students taught?" However, in seeking to make this evaluation, Ofsted uses a number of criteria which are relevant to the developing teacher.

In determining their judgements, inspectors consider the extent to which teachers:

- show good subject knowledge and understanding in the way they present and discuss their subject
- are technically competent in teaching basic skills
- plan effectively, setting clear objectives that pupils understand
- challenge and inspire pupils, expecting the most of them, so as to deepen their knowledge and understanding
- use methods which enable all pupils to learn effectively
- manage pupils well and insist on high standards of behaviour
- use time, support staff and other resources, especially information and communications technology, effectively
- assess pupils' work thoroughly and use assessments to help and encourage pupils to overcome difficulties
- use homework effectively to reinforce and /or extend what is learned in school.

This is a long list and the next part of the chapter reflects on the idea of a good teacher and how this has changed over time.

TASK 1

Developing subject knowledge

In this first task, we reflect on the nature of subject knowledge and how a teacher demonstrates good subject knowledge and understanding. Answer the following questions.

1 How do teachers show good subject knowledge and understanding in the way they present and discuss their subjects?

2 In relation to your own subject:

- what elements make up the subject?
- what are the future developments of the subject?
- what are the particular difficulties associated with the teaching of the subject?

Applebee (1989) discusses the nature of teaching as scholarship. He reflects on the image of the necessary preparation for teaching as stressing the importance of knowledge of content, e.g. in the case of an English teacher, of literature. On the face of it, arguments for the importance of such knowledge are unassailable; we can hardly teach a subject we do not know about. The issue here is of a different nature; it concerns the role of such knowledge in school teaching.

However, in the example of language studies, Applebee reflects on the past 20 years as having been particularly fruitful, as they have been for the study of child development in general. The theories of Piaget, Vygotsky, Bruner and others have become widely known, and with them emerged the image of a child as an active participant in the process of construction of knowledge. Approaches to reading instruction, for example, were transformed as teachers and scholars became aware of the complex processes of comprehension and understanding that go into a reader's or writer's approach to text. Rather than focusing on the accuracy of the final product, process-oriented approaches to instruction have sought to provide support for the young learner still in the process of solving the problems posed by a particular reading or writing task.

As in language studies we have learned more about the processes of language and learning, we have been developing a third body of knowledge to compete with generic teaching skills and traditional subject scholarship for a place in the teacher-education curriculum. This body of knowledge is *subject specific knowledge of teaching*. In the case of English teaching, this subject-specific knowledge is based on scholarship in a variety of fields, but the form it takes is different. In its most useful form, the subject-specific knowledge of English teaching is practical knowledge of the nature of children's English skills, the directions of growth these skills will follow, and the contexts that foster such growth. Applebee gives as an example knowledge of the kinds of literature 12 year olds are likely to find difficult, how they make sense of specific works when they read them, and how teachers can structure classroom activities to develop new skills and strategies that may make initially difficult works accessible.

In this form subject-specific knowledge of teaching looks very different from knowledge of a traditional subject matter. The concerns of the scholar – whether those concerns focus on the theories of literary criticism or structure of language

– are different from the concerns of the classroom teacher. Bennett (1987) thinks that the characterisation of knowledge is difficult methodologically and attempts to represent it by semantic and planning networks and flowcharts. However, the heavy demands made on teachers' knowledge structures to select and set tasks, diagnose pupil conceptions, teach cognitive processes, and manipulate complex learning environments for classes of children requires many of a teacher's actions to become routine. These routine actions simplify the complexity of the teaching task and reduce the cognitive load and ensure the teacher can pay more attention to the substantive activities and goals of teaching.

Professional development through research

As a middle manager, there is a need to reflect on the nature of subject knowledge and how it impacts on the development of teaching excellence. A key feature of educational research over the recent years has been the involvement of teachers. Whilst there have always been opportunities for teachers to engage in research as part of diploma and higher degree courses, Information Communication Technology (ICT) makes the involvement of a wider range of teachers possible. However, the nature of educational research has changed. The earlier articles to which we have referred have focused on the seminal and universal aspects of research. However, the practice of ethnographic research has illustrated the difficulty in constructing theory based on one study; it is a body of knowledge.

What is the future for educational research and how can middle managers develop this as part of their professional development? At a conference in March 2000, Professor Pring (University of Oxford, Department of Educational Studies) asked the question 'How can research be useful?' The context of the recent debate has been about developing teaching as a research or evidence-based profession. Traditionally, the model has been one in which universities carry out research and relevant findings are then applied to schools. There has been widespread criticism of research, particularly in the Hillage Report (1998). Some of the criticisms that have been levelled are that research is fragmented, inaccessible to practitioners, written by and for academics, published in journals that few read and above all, it does not answer the questions of interest to practitioners.

A key development has been the comparison with advances in the medical field. Here there is a similar emphasis on evidence-based practice. The Cochrane Centre sets out to provide extensive reviews of all research evidence in a particular medical field. Medical practitioners and researchers work together to identify the issues to be reviewed. The outcomes of the reviews are intended to provide evidence to assist in the making of professional judgements – not to provide prescriptions for practice.

An approach like this offers two significant potential benefits. The first is that engaging in research enterprises could be a key source of professional satisfaction and could enhance the standing of those involved in education. The other is that it could result in the bringing together of interested individuals and institutions into professional communities.

Past ideas of a 'good' teacher

The idea of the 'good teacher' has varied over time. Successive policies have offered very different, even contradictory views of the teacher. Proposals which have come from governments, Ofsted, a reform group or a professional association will often have had different, even diametrically opposed, images of the teachers necessary to carry out their proposals. Teachers working within ensuing projects will have developed skills, knowledge and even career choices which differentiate their idea of a 'good teacher' from that of their colleagues.

An early example of a curriculum statement which contains within it a strong enhanced version of the teacher and the curriculum, which is often referred to by curriculum historians because of its actual or symbolic influence over teachers' work, is contained in the *Handbook of Suggestions for Teachers*. The *Handbook* was produced, and then revised, several times during the course of the last century by the Board or Ministry of Education, from 1904 right through to one version, *Primary Education*, in 1959. Although the *Handbook* contained detailed arguments for curriculum practice and teachers were expected always to have a copy within reach, the preface implied a more liberal, even liberated view of 'the good teacher'.

> *'The only uniformity of practice that the Board of Education desire to see in the teaching of Public Elementary schools is that each teacher shall think for himself and work out for himself such methods of teaching as may use his powers to the best advantage and be best suited to the particular needs and conditions of the school ... freedom implies a corresponding responsibility in its use.'*

The strength of the statement should really be judged against the common view of the elementary school teacher which prevailed in the early decades of the twentieth century, which may be characterised as underpaid drudgery performed by poorly educated men and women of low social status. Yet 'good teachers' are now seen as individuals who think about and define their practice in relation to local conditions whilst recognising their responsibility in relation to the government.

Skilbeck (1989) suggested that the good teacher was characterised by:

1 The teacher's pedagogical practice will be an area of *that individual's* skill and decision making.

2 Pedagogy and content will be regularly updated to ensure improvement in several areas of the curriculum (learning skills, standards, morality, etc.). Updating will occur through regular guidelines and directions in the curriculum.

3 Assessment in the classroom will be a new skill area to be mastered by teachers who will in turn need to know about the performance indicators applied to them.

4 The teacher will recognise the sensitivity of their work in the public and political context and will need to explain themselves and to negotiate/consult with parents and other sections of the community and to make their curriculum link with the work place and the community.

5 The teacher will operate within flexible staffing structures to allow for changes of national priority and economic stringency.

'Good teachers' will work within their classrooms and schools on the effective implementation of national curriculum guidelines by means of improved pedagogy, regular knowledge base updating and the new techniques of assessment. 'Good teachers' will recognise that they work in an education service that has a concentration of control and policy and that it is their duty to work efficiently within national guidelines and to consult local parents, employers and other community members.

Cohen and Manion (1977) describe successful teachers as those who reflected the following elements in their teaching:

- they varied their classroom role from dominative to supportive spontaneously and were able to secure both students' compliance and initiative as the situation demanded
- they could switch at will from one role to another and did not blindly follow a single approach to the exclusion of other approaches
- they were able to move easily from diagnosing a classroom problem to suggesting a follow-up course of action
- they were able to be both critical of their classroom pupils and sensitive to their needs as human beings.

Briefly, successful teachers are flexible in their teaching styles and can shift easily and naturally from the direct to the indirect, from being critical observers to sympathetic counsellors, depending on the need.

The perceptual differences between good and poor teachers investigated by Combs (1965) suggest that good teachers can be distinguished from poor ones with respect to the following perceptions about other people:

- Good teachers are more likely to have an internal rather than an external frame of reference. That is, they seek to understand how things seem to others and then use this as a guide for their own behaviour.

- Good teachers are more concerned with people and their reactions than with things and events.

- Good teachers are more concerned with the subjective-perceptual experience of people than with objective events. They are, again, more concerned with how things seem to people than just the so-called or alleged facts.

- Good teachers seek to understand the causes of people's behaviours in terms of their current thinking, feelings, beliefs and understandings rather than in terms of forces exerted on them now or in the past.

- Good teachers generally trust other people and perceive them as having the capacity to solve their own problems.

- Good teachers see others as being friendly and enhancing rather than hostile or threatening.

- Good teachers tend to see other people as being of worth. They show regard for a person's dignity and integrity.

- Good teachers see people as their behaviours and essentially developing from within rather than as a product of external events to be moulded or directed. In other words, they see people as creative and dynamic rather than passive or inert.

Good teachers bring about effective learning

More particularly, however, MacGilchrist, Myers and Reed (1997) take a view that the effectiveness of teaching is defined in terms of the learning that takes place. For school learning to be enhanced and effective they argue that teachers need to understand the different factors that can influence a pupil's motivation and ability to learn. To do this, they suggest, that teachers need to be:

- knowledgeable about learning as a process

- knowledgeable about learners and

- knowledgeable about what learners want.

One feature which distinguishes new ways of thinking about the effectiveness of the learning process is the focus of attention on the learners themselves. MacGilchrist et al. argue that learners are vital to the learning process. This at first reading seems an obvious point.

Bowring-Carr and West-Burnham (1997) discuss the need for schools to change as organisations. The school that they describe is a place where learning is at the centre of the organisation; it is not a school coming from science fiction, but one which is not too far from what some schools are striving towards today. They suggest that there needs to be more thinking on the schools of the future. One aspect of our system and its reluctance to change is the number of teachers who ask that there be no more change for a while. They are suffering, or so they claim, from an excess of change, and suggest that they are given time for all the upheavals of the last few years to bed down and become routine. There is, Bowring-Carr and West-Burnham, argue, no such option. In a world of stability, or at least one of gradual and predictable change, it might have been possible for an institution to remain static and survive. In this world of ever increasing quantitative change, and change occurring at increasing speed, schools (and therefore teachers) have a stark choice. They can either change, adapting themselves to the new demands and expectations of their students, or they do not change, and therefore decline in credibility, usefulness and relevance.

The focus of this chapter is to identify those features of a teacher's work which make for excellence.

Quality of teaching – lesson observation

Table 1.1 below is a checklist of the criteria used by Ofsted when assessing the quality of teaching.

TABLE 1.1 Ofsted criteria for assessing the quality of teaching

Context of Observation

Include: a brief description of what the teachers and pupils are doing;

a brief summary of the lesson content, activities and organisation; and

describe the role of any support staff and/or other adults present.

Evidence

Teaching: Consider the extent to which teachers:

- show good subject knowledge and understanding in the way they present and discuss their subject
- are technically competent in teaching basic skills
- plan effectively, setting clear objectives that pupils understand
- challenge and inspire pupils, expecting the most of them, so as to deepen their knowledge and understanding
- use methods which enable pupils to learn effectively
- manage pupils well and insist on high standards of behaviour
- use time, support staff and other resources, especially ICT, effectively
- assess pupils' work thoroughly and use assessments to help and encourage pupils to overcome difficulties
- use homework effectively to reinforce and/or extend what is learned at school.

Learning: Consider the extent to which pupils:

- acquire new knowledge and skills, develop ideas and increase their understanding
- apply intellectual, physical or creative effort in their work
- are productive and work at a good pace
- show interest in their work, are able to sustain their concentration and think and learn for themselves
- understand what they are doing, how well they have done and how they can improve.

Attainment: Consider, for the subject:

- what pupils know, do and understand in the different aspects of the subject
- pupils' understanding and ability to apply their knowledge to related problems
- the extent to which pupils' achievements meet or exceed the levels set by: the National Curriculum and, where applicable, the local agreed syllabus for religious education, and any examination or assessment objectives
- any differences in the standards achieved by pupils of different gender or ethnic background

- whether pupils with SEN, those having English as an additional language or those who are gifted and talented, are making good enough progress
- whether standards for the various groups of pupils are high enough.

Attitudes and behaviour: Consider the extent to which pupils:

- are keen and eager and respond well to the educational demands made on them
- behave well in lessons, and are courteous, trustworthy and show respect for property
- form constructive relationships with one another, and with teachers and other adults
- work in an atmosphere free from oppressive behaviour, such as bullying, sexism and racism
- effect on what they do and understand its impact on others
- respect other people's differences, particularly their feelings, values and beliefs
- show initiative and are willing to take responsibility.

Any other significant evidence:

Look for:

- competence in applying skills of literacy, numeracy and ICT
- any effects of staffing, resources or accommodation that impact significantly on standards and quality of work
- other issues relating to SEN, including effectiveness of support staff.

The purpose of this chapter is not to offer detailed guidance on how to become a better teacher – there are countless books which seek to do this. However, an awareness of those criteria which are judged to make one an excellent teacher is essential for the aspiring middle manager. Middle managers who are subject leaders are responsible for the quality of teaching of their subject. Middle managers who are responsible for a Key Stage or Year group will have their responsibility defined in terms of the achievement of the year group. Therefore middle managers, whatever their role, need to have a depth of understanding when considering the issues which affect the quality of teaching and learning.

An important aspect of the teacher's role, which is identified a number of times in the Ofsted criteria, is the role of support staff and other adults. The emphasis on social inclusion and the reduction in the number of special school places has brought this issue to the fore. In developing teaching skill the emphasis that is placed on the learning needs of students is clearly paramount.

Differentiation

Differentiation is a perennial challenge for all teachers. Bowring-Carr and West-Burnham (1997) describe the need for confidence that every individual is learning as being a key factor. If the teaching received by students is to be described as being of quality, then they argue, it has to be 'bespoke'. However, choice is severely constrained in schools – therefore, effective learning requires choice in *how* pupils learn rather than *what* they learn. A first step is to identify the variables of learning that have to be managed. Bowring-Carr and West-Burnham's list of variables is as follows:

- Learning styles
- Teaching strategies
- Prior knowledge
- Cognitive skills
- Social skills
- Feedback, recognition and reinforcement
- Neurological factors
- Health and diet
- Access to resources
- Intrinsic motivation
- Multiple intelligences
- Information technology.

This is a long list and it underlines the increasingly complex role that the teacher has to try to fulfil. Chapter 5 in Bowring-Carr and West-Burnham (1997) is recommended as further reading on this important topic. However, there are particular features of this list that are to be explored within the context of differentiated learning.

TASK 2

Preparing to differentiate a topic

In this task you are asked to consider what constitutes differentiated work in your subject area and how you can create a 'bespoke' lesson.

Think of a topic that you know well and have taught to a class recently. Think of a class you know well. Identify five students across the ability range within that class (if it is a set, the issue is still pertinent). Identify the different elements of the topic.

- What are the learning outcomes for this topic?
- What prior knowledge did you presume?
- What was your starting point for the topic?
- What assessment did you plan for this topic and at what stage did it inform your planning?

There are some challenging issues to discuss in this activity and we take them in turn.

The ability to identify the different elements of a topic is a critical factor when planning a teaching programme. The effective teacher needs to be able to break the topic down into a range of learning units. The following table illustrates the way in which a French teacher breaks down the topic of food for a Year 8 class.

TABLE 1.2 Topic analysis: skills, outcomes, methods

Topic: Food and Drink

Skills	Outcomes	Methods
Know the names of a range of snack foods from a café or fast-food place	Students can: – Speak the words of a range of foods – Write and spell correctly the words and associated phrases	■ Flashcards ■ Drawings ■ Vocabulary lists ■ Tests on words and phrases ■ Listening to tape recording ■ Making recordings
Know the names for fruit and vegetables	Students can: – Speak the words and phrases for different fruits and vegetables – Write and spell correctly the words and associated phrases	■ Flashcards ■ Drawings ■ Vocabulary lists ■ Tests on words and phrases ■ Listening to tape recording ■ Making recordings
Be able to hold a conversation where a student can buy a range of foods	Students can: – Say the appropriate phrases both as a buyer and seller	The above plus video recordings, use of artefacts, etc.

What Table 1.2 illustrates is that by breaking the topic down into a number of elements, the teacher is able to plan a learning programme for pupils. The noteworthy feature of this method is that it identifies at the start what it is the student has to be able to do by the end of the unit of work. This is important because it will enable the teacher to plan the teaching with the learning outcomes in mind. The process is one where the learning needs are identified, the assessment outcomes are specified and the teaching activities are planned to address these needs and outcomes. The focus for the teacher is not about what he or she is planning to teach but about what students are going to learn. By making this important paradigm shift, the teacher is empowered to plan with learning (rather than teaching) at the fore.

Further by breaking down the topic even more and considering the learning outcomes in greater depth, the planning of the learning becomes, in our view, more proactive and more straightforward. It is possible to plan the unit lesson by lesson. Therefore, a planning document for such a unit of work can include the items listed in Table 1.3.

TABLE 1.3 Topic analysis: planning document model

1 Lesson by lesson objectives

2 Lesson outcomes and assessment objectives

3 Learning activities

4 Teaching strategies

5 Resources

6 Homework tasks which enhance the learning in class

7 Timing and pace

By moving towards this model for planning work, the prospect of differentiation becomes a more realistic one. Why? There are two reasons. The first is that the hard work of planning the outcomes of the lessons is done in advance. This enables all those involved in delivering the curriculum to see how it fits together – it brings coherence and cohesion. Second, it facilitates quality planning – it means that the teacher can think about the learning needs of each student in the class. The need for assessment is highlighted in this strategy – it emphasises that if a lesson is to be a valuable learning experience for the students then it needs to be pitched appropriately. By making assessment one of the priorities, this is then made a realistic possibility.

Planning work with students in mind

When planning a unit of work it is helpful to picture the students who will be taught. This is where the issue of differentiation comes once more to the fore.

In schools where there is a setting policy, there is sometimes an assumption that the issue of differentiation has been addressed. This in some ways represents the shift that needs to occur. There has to be an acknowledgement that children have individual learning needs and that it is the role of the classroom teacher to act as a *learning agent*. However, by thinking of students in the class who represent the range of ability it is possible to start to produce a differentiated lesson within the parameters of five groups.

TASK 3

Selecting a strategy for differentiation

The following task is designed to help you to consider the priority and strategies that might be employed to produce a differentiated programme.

In Table 1.4 below are ten statements about differentiation. Decide whether each statement relates to input (what the teacher does), process (the work the students do) or outcome (the work that is assessed).

Use the statements and produce a rank order of importance.

Justify your ranking.

TABLE 1.4 Ten differentiation strategies

1 All the students in my classes work at their own level on different assignments, within a given topic.

2 I divide my class into ability groups and each group does different work on the same topic.

3 I teach to the middle of my classes – all my students work on the same assignments.

4 All the students complete common assignments but there is extension work for the most able.

5 Students select tasks for themselves.

6 I structure the work so that the most able students progress quickly through the first parts of the assignments and progress to the harder material.

7 I differentiate through output rather than input.

8 Students work on common assignments but help one another.

9 Students work through the same exercises but at different rates – I differentiate through the work rate.

10 All students attempt some aspects of the same topic but then have guided choices through a range of differentiated tasks.

The consequence of differentiating by input process or outcome has implications for the middle manager thinking of developing a teaching programme.

TABLE 1.5 Input, process and outcome differentiation – benefits and consequences

Statement	Benefits of the approach	Consequences of the approach
Input	■ The students tackle work appropriately matched to their ability. ■ Possibility of assessment related to the input is enhanced. ■ A wide range of media can be utilised. ■ Resources can be planned around such matters as readability, ease of use by students.	■ At this stage the input needs to be carefully classified. ■ The teacher needs accurate baseline data on which to base the judgement. ■ Takes time to create high quality resources – 10 hours of teacher preparation time to produce one hour of student work.
Process	■ Students benefit from learning new skills and knowledge before they tackle assignments. ■ Study skills can be enhanced because they are introduced within a specific context. ■ A variety of tasks can be produced. ■ The process can be adapted readily to take account of progress.	■ Students may not fulfil expectations if the process matching is inaccurate. ■ The variety of tasks can reduce teacher efficiency. ■ Careful monitoring is required to ensure that students make appropriate progress.

Statement	Benefits of the approach	Consequences of the approach
	■ Mechanisms can be built in to help students stay on task.	
Outcome	■ Course objectives can be planned to be accessible to all. ■ The assessment depends entirely on the outcome. ■ No stigmatisation of students tackling different work. ■ Response reflects what student has achieved. ■ Students can exceed expectations.	■ Close monitoring will be needed to ensure adequate challenge for the most able and realistic challenges for the least able.

Leading and managing projects

An essential part of an aspiring middle manager's development is the leading and managing of projects. Certainly, in terms of a job application, it is essential that you have led successfully a range of projects to conclusion.

The features of a good project in this context are:

1 There is a clearly defined need for the project – probably identified by pupil data or response.

2 The project leader has identified the overall strategy by the outcomes that will result from the successful implementation of the project.

3 The project leader has negotiated a plan with the management team (or the current team leader). This plan contains details such as budget, time plans and stage outcomes (i.e. at specified times during the project, there will be outcomes which contribute to the whole effort). This section is about leading a project and working with others.

Establishing a contract

If this process is to be effective and the benefits maximised there needs to be a clear contract. There are several stages to this.

1 *Negotiating the task.* The original idea may spring from a team meeting, the team leader presenting some ideas to the team, the development plan or a chance meeting. Whatever the starting point, you need to consider what outcomes are required and how feasible the aims of the project are. It may be that you are very keen to pursue a particular topic but the team leader does not agree. This needs to be tackled sensitively and you need to consider the reasons for the project carefully and seek to persuade the team leader or manager.

One possible means is to discuss with the team leader exactly what is necessary to complete the task. One outcome of such a discussion might be that you accept that the job is beyond your skill – at this time. However, if the team leader is able to support you and give strong and positive direction, then much can be achieved.

2 *Deciding what to do.* For any job to be done there are stages. These include, as a minimum:

- *Planning* – this is where the job is broken down into its essential parts. An audit of what is current practice may be necessary. One outcome should be a statement of intent and purpose. This should include a timescale.

- *Process* – this is where the job is actually done. This may include negotiating with individuals, creating resources, presenting information, reporting findings, etc. The main outcome is that the task is completed.

- *Evaluation* – no process is complete without some evaluation of what has been done. This may simply be a reflection of what went well, what was less successful. For a developmental task, the evaluation should also include a consideration of how the teacher has planned and carried out the task. Where the work has involved leading and managing others, time should be given for you to reflect on your interpersonal skills.

- *Review* – this is an essential part of the cycle. This needs to include a conclusion on the task and recommendation on how the work could be developed in the future. At the basic level, it is about how the job should be carried out next time.

3 *Timing and reporting on progress.* An important part of the process is to agree a timescale. The timing should complement the plan and there should be identifiable outcomes. This negotiation is an important means of providing support for the teacher. Also, it will enable the work of the team to be kept to time.

4 *Supporting the teacher.* The process outlined above is the means by which you (the teacher) are supported. The team leader and you agree the outcomes and the timing. Thus, the team leader is in a position to offer the appropriate amount of support. Experienced staff, operating within their 'comfort zone' may need little guidance – they can be directed and then can 'get on with it'. Others need more.

5 *Learning from the job.* The process of working together has to be a developmental one and time for reflection is important to the future work of the team. It is also worthwhile for you to reflect on the teachers' response to your direction. Has the amount of direction and guidance been appropriate? Further, how might you continue the developmental process with the team as a whole and the teachers as individuals?

Delegation

The practice of delegation is a fundamental one. Team leaders have a responsibility, not only to the team, but also to themselves to delegate effectively. If a team is to act in cohort, then opportunities for them to collaborate are essential. The processes outlined in this chapter provide the teacher with a framework that not only encourages teamwork, but also makes it inescapable. This is a feature that is worthy of reflection.

At the start of this section, we referred to the need to develop people, not only to maximise the effectiveness of the team, but also as a wider responsibility to the profession as a whole. Many teachers will move schools in order to gain promotion. Teachers as individuals and schools as organisations benefit from the cross-fertilisation of ideas that this system inevitably brings. However, much is lost when an experienced teacher finds it necessary to leave the school to obtain the promotion he/she desires. It is desirable within the system that there should be an element of succession planning. The team leader can use his/her vision for the team to develop a successor. Indeed the Green paper on Teachers' Pay and Conditions may provide greater opportunities for advancement within the existing structure. Initiatives such as Advanced Skills Teachers, the Leadership Scale, the Threshold Assessment to name but three, offer scope for an organisation to develop a policy which provides opportunities for teachers to progress within the organisation. Therefore, to maximise these possibilities, the team leader should see the team within the context of successors whilst recognising there will be those who do not want the promotion, the Threshold Assessment, and all that goes with it.

As well as the teaching responsibilities of the professionals, schools and colleges still need to have management tasks carried out. The tasks include setting and monitoring budgets, resourcing teaching and learning, providing a well-qualified and competent staff, liaising with students, parents, employers and the wider community, and responding to government requirements. Responsibility for these tasks can be concentrated in the hands of a small number of people or widely dispersed among the staff.

However senior or junior their formal position in the organisation may be, managers are both agents of change and bulwarks against it. In a stable environment, their role is one of continuing review and improvement. In turbulent times, they may have to filter the pressures created by demands for change so that those who work in their area of responsibility can carry on in as secure an environment as possible. Good management involves supporting colleagues and assisting them with resources and staff development opportunities to cope with the changes that are required. And, uncomfortable though it may be sometimes, it requires monitoring and evaluating their own work and that of others so that standards are maintained and, when possible, improved.

All this requires of managers an understanding of how organisations work, how people are motivated, and how change can be brought about successfully. It requires an awareness of the tasks of leadership. And it requires the ability to investigate problems and issues within their area of responsibility and, if necessary, more widely, in order to generate new ideas and approaches which can keep the organisation operating well and delivering what is required.

_____ Being a life-long learner _____

As an individual, you may have a need to find out the information – or find the knowledge or expertise that is possessed by a colleague. The importance of management courses such as the MA degree, is emphasised by the need for organisations to continue along the road of self-review and continuous improvement.

The Study Guide to the Open University's MA course 'Educational Management in Action' sets out well the reasons why an aspirant middle manager should consider further study. The Study Guide states the aims of the course as:

> '... to develop your skills of investigation and reflection in order to improve your own management practice and assist others to improve theirs.'

This statement emphasises our assertion that the motivation for such a course of study should be about improving one's professional practice. This is achieved through developing a theoretical basis for the management practices that are developed. Further, the need for reflection is espoused: the leader and manager of the future needs to be someone who can research a problem and when a solution is proposed can reflect on the strategy and the practices involved. This is the virtue of such courses: the opportunity to develop an in-depth understanding and to articulate theories on leadership and management is essential training for the practitioner.

Some people will baulk at the idea of lots of bookwork and essay writing. The choice of the most appropriate course is key. Most Masters courses will have a taught element assessed through coursework assignments, examinations and dissertations. Some courses, however, will be structured to accommodate the needs of the modern schoolteacher; frequently, managers will want reports on issues, rather than an essay. Therefore, courses such as the OU MA have incorporated this into the assessment process; there is an emphasis on reflective practice, action research and management style reports.

One of the benefits of extended study is a greater understanding of the issues that face managers and this is the basis for improving practice. What enables the teacher to move into management is an understanding of the need for management and the principles of management. When considering the move to middle management, the individual has to consider what kind of model they will embody. What will be the principles on which they will act? To do this, there has to come first an understanding of the issues of school management and leadership.

The idea of learning management theory is attractive to some people in its own right. However, for the majority, there needs to be point to the task. Doing further study is hard work – coming home after a day's teaching to the prospect of three hours academic study is quite a daunting prospect. However, if the aim of the course is to improve one's ability to apply knowledge of educational management to daily life and to reflect on this knowledge – the task becomes easier.

However, the prospect of further study needs to be considered carefully. Whilst the outcome is desirable (in that it increases management potential and prepares one for more senior positions) the prospect of the work is not always so attractive. There are a number of issues to consider:

- support from school
- support from home
- financial implications
- managing the time.

The benefits of further study should not just be confined to the individual. If you want to embark on a course of study that is designed to improve your professional practice then it is proper to discuss this with a member of the senior team. Often, they will have done further study themselves and so will be aware of the task being undertaken. Engaging their support is important because, if there is a need for additional information, then early discussion will help to ease the way. Also, if the school can foresee a benefit then there are ways in which it can provide support in the form of timetabling (perhaps blocking time for the teacher to study), mentoring and possibly, helping with negotiations with other staff. In some cases, there may be financial assistance for the cost of fees.

A number of the writers of this series have undertaken such courses. It is essential that a partner is aware of the implications before the course begins. In taking on additional work, there is a clear need for time to be spent; this may be at the expense of caring for children or attending to the myriad of domestic responsibilities that we take on. Also, if there is no financial support from the school, there are fees to be paid and the course to be resourced. These matters need to be discussed and planned.

The benefits of professional study are immense and are not only confined to those explored above. By planning a course of study which involves researching an issue, one becomes adept at managing one's time. Having to consider a range of tasks – preparing for lessons, marking books, reading a book on management, having a relationship – these are all part of the modern teacher's life. The opportunity to develop time management strategies is a lesson well learnt and one which stands us in good stead as we progress.

Starting to look for a post

As time progresses and you acquire experience, you will start to look for a post. It is important that at the planning stage, you are aware of the skills and attributes that are required for this job.

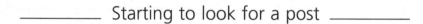

TASK 4

Analysing a job description

When posts are advertised it is customary to provide candidates with a job description. Below is reproduced a job description for the Head of Mathematics in a large comprehensive school. This task is designed to enable you to identify the skills and experiences needed for the post.

Read the job description for the Head of Mathematics. Using this document identify:

- the core purpose and its implications

- the key attributes that are being sought by the school

- how a teacher can plan to meet these attributes.

TABLE 1.6   Job description for a Head of Mathematics

The Head of Mathematics is responsible for all aspects of Mathematics in the school.

Accountable to: Deputy Headteacher

Core Purpose of the Subject Leader

The core purpose of a Head of Mathematics is to provide professional leadership and management for a subject to secure high quality teaching, effective use of resources and improved standards of learning and achievement for all pupils. A copy of the National Standards for Subject Leaders forms part of this Job Description.

The specific tasks associated with the role of Head of Mathematics are the:

Strategic Direction of Mathematics

The tasks associated with the role of Head of Mathematics are specifically to:

- *Lead the development and implementation of policies and practices in line with School policies.*

- *Advise the Headteacher and Deputy Headteacher of developments in Mathematics.*

- *Develop and ensure the effective delivery of ICT as part of Mathematics portfolio.*

- *Prepare development plans as necessary.*

- *Promote Mathematics in school and beyond.*

- *Produce reports for the Headteacher and Deputy Headteacher, as required.*

- *Lead the development of a Numeracy Policy for the school.*

Teaching and Learning of Mathematics

The tasks associated with the role of Head of Mathematics are specifically to:

- *Implement school policy on monitoring and evaluating the work of the departments. This will include undertaking lesson observation, giving feedback to staff and where appropriate setting targets to improve the quality of teaching.*

- *Lead the production and updating of schemes of work. These should ensure curriculum coverage, continuity and progression in the Mathematics for all pupils, including those of high ability and those with special needs.*

- *Coordinate the production of tests and examinations, of the appropriate standard across Mathematics area.*

- *Keep parents well informed about their child's achievement in Mathematics and ensure that all information sent to parents is of a high standard.*

- *Ensure that all pupils are prepared adequately for public examinations.*

Leading and Managing Staff

The tasks associated with the role of Head of Mathematics are specifically to:

- *Direct and supervise the work of teachers delivering Mathematics.*

- *Lead the production of the Subject Handbook and update it regularly.*

- *Create and sustain a team of teachers, who have detailed job descriptions, which set out their responsibilities and duties.*

- *Provide information and participate in Threshold Assessment and Performance Management processes.*

Efficient and Effective deployment of staff and resources

The tasks associated with the role of Head of Mathematics are specifically to:

- *Be responsible for the health and safety of the designated subject rooms.*

- *Manage the delegated budget for Mathematics and to manage the resources efficiently.*

And to undertake any other duties, as required.

The core purpose is stated at the start of the document and it is taken from the National Standards for Subject Leaders. There are a number of key attributes that are stated in this job description and these are:

- leading and developing – this relates to the production of policies and also to the work of the team

- responsibility

- managing, directing and supervising

- coordinating and implementing.

These skills and attributes are essential for the middle manager. These can be acquired through a range of projects and initiatives.

The most important characteristic of the aspirant middle manager is to be an excellent teacher. By focusing attention on this aspect of their work and developing projects around this core function, the teacher will be in a strong position to take on responsibility in whatever form it is offered.

Summary

At some point in your career you need to think through what you want to do in the long term. Whether you are keen to progress to middle management or simply prepare for threshold assessment the key features are:

- set the goal of becoming an excellent teacher

- learn the qualities which Ofsted seek when making judgements

- incorporate these features into classroom practice

- focus on getting the teaching and learning right before looking beyond the classroom

- choose projects which directly impact on pupil achievement

- establish a clear remit for the project and agree a contract

- take the opportunity to work alongside others on projects and invite them to join you on yours

- seek out feedback and use it to develop your expertise

- look at the next job – see what skills and attributes are required and plan for them

- think years ahead – teachers who invest in their schools and in themselves will always grow as professionals.

chapter two

Making the application and preparing for interview

Core purposes

Professionalism

Motivation

Information sources

Planning an application

Summary

In Chapter 1 we discussed how the aspiring middle manager should prepare for this role. In this chapter we outline the process of making an application and preparing for an interview. Because of the strategic importance of the middle manager in a school, the appointment process is thorough and testing.

In this chapter we seek to outline the process, and the tasks are designed to help you to understand more about the role and the rationale which underpins this process. This chapter is divided into sections which deal with:

- questions to ask before making an application – why do you want to do the job?
- the National Standards for Subject Leaders
- the core purpose of the subject leader
- the role of the middle manager in school
- motives for being a middle manager
- finding out information about the advertised post
- reading a person specification
- reading a job description
- writing a letter of application and completing an application form
- writing a curriculum vitae (CV)
- interview preparation
- questions to consider
- accepting the post.

Core purposes

Before making any application for a middle management post in education, teachers have to ask themselves some serious questions. The role of the middle manager in schools has changed considerably over the past few years and is set to change more radically over the next couple of years. There are a number of national initiatives which have brought about this change and will be responsible for driving the additional elements of the middle manager's job. Anyone contemplating the move to middle management needs to consider the additional demands of the job and assess for themselves the impact that they believe it will have on them as a professional and as a person.

A crucial document to read at this stage is the National Standards for Subject Leaders. This document, published by the Teacher Training Agency (TTA) sets out the personal and professional requirements of a subject leader. However, whilst this document is about *subject* leadership, the following discussion and tasks will develop ideas for a teacher preparing to make an application for any middle management role.

The main aims of the standards are to set out the knowledge, understanding, skills and attributes which relate to the key areas of subject leadership. The standards define expertise in subject leadership and are designed to guide the professional development of teachers aiming to increase their effectiveness as subject leaders or of those aspiring to take responsibility for leading the subject.

Core purpose of the subject leader

The opening statement of the National Standards articulates the core purpose, as follows:

> 'The core purpose of the Subject Leader is to provide professional leadership for a subject to secure high quality teaching, effective use of resources and improved standards of learning for all pupils.'

TASK 5

The meaning of the core purpose statement

There are four key phrases in the above statement of core purpose. Using Table 2.1 as a guide, explain what you think is meant by these phrases.

TABLE 2.1 Analysis of the core purpose of a subject leader

Core purpose phrase	Questions to consider	Your response
1. Provide professional leadership	■ Is the word 'provide' significant for you? Does this give you an indication of the nature of your role? ■ What are the features of being a 'professional' in the educational context? ■ Is your definition of a professional specific to the phase of education in which you work: Junior, Middle, Secondary, Special, FE? ■ What do you understand by the term 'leadership'? ■ In what ways does your practice embody 'leadership'?	
2. Secure high quality teaching	■ What does the word 'secure' imply for you in this role? ■ What defines 'high quality teaching'? ■ What experience have you of judging the teaching of others? ■ What does Ofsted have to say on the subject of high quality teaching?	
3. Secure effective use of resources	■ As a middle manager, you will have some budgetary responsibility. What is your attitude to public money? ■ How will you allocate resources in your management role? ■ What is effectiveness? How does efficiency fit in with your ideas?	
4. Secure improved standards of learning for all pupils	■ How do you measure improvement? ■ What is quantitative improvement? ■ What is qualitative improvement? ■ How do you define learning?	

These are big questions and need serious consideration. However, they illustrate both the enormity of the task of middle management and the level of responsibility that is placed on the teacher appointed. To consider these issues in more detail, however, will enable us to see how skills and attributes can be fitted to this core purpose.

What is educational provision? – A historical perspective

The word 'provide' is a significant one in this context. The nature of education has changed: we refer to educational 'provision'. The function of schools is to provide an education. This is a significant shift from the charitable initiatives of the early schools. The function of the early public school education was to facilitate a young man's entrée into the professions and the idea of 'provision' is certainly a considerable movement away from this. In many ways, the idea of provision is a utilitarian idea where schooling is designed to prepare children for their adult roles. There is an expectation that education will be provided and that teachers are the providers – it is a function. The functionalist model could lead to some kind of guarantee – the movement in educational establishments to gaining quality marks (such as Investor in People, Kite Marks, Beacon School status, etc.) is perhaps a form of this. The quality marks are an attempt to embody the quality provision that the school offers. A school which has these marks has taken this issue seriously.

Being a modern subject leader

What does this mean for the middle manager? For the aspiring subject leader it means the following:

- The curriculum is delivered equitably – there should be schemes of work which map out the entire curriculum coverage for the subject.

- The team is led in a professional manner. This means that there are policies which address such matters as assessment, equal opportunities, behaviour, etc. Further, these are policies in practice – they are part of the daily life in the school and are monitored effectively.

- The subject leader has a vision for the subject – the middle manager is secure in the place of the subject in the curriculum and knows how to realise his/her vision.

Professionalism

The word 'professional' has been subjected to considerable misuse over recent years. For many, a professional is someone who does the job and gets paid for it! We hear of the professional footballer, the professional rugby player to name but two. However, some attributes of the more traditional professions give us insight into the principle of the 'professional teacher'.

TABLE 2.2 **Attributes of some of the professions**

Profession	Attribute	Implications for the teacher
Medicine	■ Expectation that the professional will continue to develop professionally. ■ Pre-registration period before a doctor is fully qualified to practise. ■ Professional body which represents and regulates the profession.	■ Some teachers continue their professional development by undertaking Master degree courses, etc; however such are in a minority. This is particularly the case where time and funding have been reduced or removed. ■ The teachers' associations are, in the main, trade unions, which have a representative but not a regulatory function.
Law	■ Candidates for the profession take articles or pupillage – there is an expectation that their professional competence will be acquired over a period of time. ■ Pupils assist the barrister in preparing for cases. ■ Service and expertise is recognised by the award of Queens Counsel status.	■ There is a stated belief that the art of advocacy has to be acquired and learnt from the more experienced. ■ The practice of the law is one where the lawyer's skill is rehearsed and guided. ■ Experience is valued and recognised.
Clergy	■ A young cleric will act as a curate under the direction of an experienced priest.	■ Recognition that the clergy is vocational. It is a commitment to the faith and to the role of the clergy in society.

Although the attributes are carefully selected, and it would be naïve to believe that it is as straightforward as these attributes suggest – there are important implications for teachers.

We shall now consider the features of being a 'professional' in the educational context. There are a number of elements which should be included.

What it means to be a professional teacher

First, the commitment to updating and developing subject knowledge. In the main, the subject knowledge acquired as part of a first degree is beyond that expected of a schoolteacher. However, there are a significant number of teachers who have not learnt ICT skills; also, there is often a need for staff to be redeployed and new skills are required. The culture needs to be one where teachers expect to develop their subject knowledge. Further, there is a need for teachers to develop their leadership and management skills. Whilst there is no substitute for experience, any reflection is enhanced when underpinned by theory. This is the value of Masters degrees which specialise in Management in Education. However, more will be said of this elsewhere in the book.

The recent appointment of a Chairman of the Teaching Council is for many long overdue. The remit of the Teaching Council is to be a forum for educational debate and many would see the Council as developing its brief to include regulation. The database held on teachers is surely the first step in this process.

Second, there is a recognition among teachers that skills take time to acquire. A useful metaphor for a teacher's career is that of a marathon rather than a sprint. The rhythm of the academic year means that certain issues emerge only once a year. For example, when preparing students for public examinations, teachers employ a range of strategies to help their students to retain and apply the knowledge they have acquired. Particular difficulties can arise with any strategy – a reflective teacher may consider the solution but will not be able to test it out until it recurs, perhaps the following year. There may be procedural issues which do not emerge until the system is tried out, for example, Options systems at Key Stage 4, arrangements for Key Stage tests, etc.; again these events occur annually. For some professionals, issues may arise once in a professional lifetime and the opportunity for reflection may not benefit the process directly. A Year Head may have to deal with the death of a child. For most teachers this is a very rare occurrence. It will require sound skills and will test the school as an organisation and the teacher as a professional. However, the middle manager may never need to call on these skills again. However, such an incident illustrates the need for professional dialogue between teachers in posts of responsibility. No one can be expected to have experienced every situation and have the perfect solution – there needs to be, in us all, a recognition, that skills and experiences are acquired and that there is a wealth of experience in every school. The older teachers are the ones with the most experience – and that needs to be both acknowledged and valued.

The definition of a professional is, in some ways, specific to the phase of education. For example, the intellectual demands made of a teacher working in a school where the vast majority go on to university, many to Oxbridge differ from those needed by a someone teaching in an education action zone. This is not to say that children attending these schools do not have intellectual needs, but the comparative demands are an issue.

TASK 6

Identifying the attributes and skills of the professional teacher

In this task you need to think about the type of professional who works in different phases of education.

Consider the intellectual attributes together with the teaching skills. If there are interpersonal skills which you consider important, note them in the spaces provided.

TABLE 2.3 Features of teachers in different educational phases

Phase of education	Features of a teacher in this phase	Implications for the middle manager
Nursery and infant	■ parenting role ■ social skills training ■ developing numeracy ■ developing literacy ■ work alone for most of the day ■ school tends to be small ■ ■ ■ ■	
Junior	■ sense of 'my class' is still prevalent	

Phase of education	Features of a teacher in this phase	Implications for the middle manager
	■ movement towards emphasis on subjects ■ preparation for next phase of education ■ schools are still small (compared with Secondary) but the team is larger ■ larger team makes for more developed hierarchy ■ ■	
Middle	■ elements of both primary and secondary education systems ■ movement towards subject specialism ■ middle schools straddle Key Stages ■ ■	
Secondary – Independent	■ often a strong sense of tradition ■ boarding schools emphasise the community aspect ■ the link between the customer and the provider is enhanced – but is complicated by the notion of 'privilege' ■ there is an expectation that a certain level of success will be achieved ■ ■	
Secondary – strong academic tradition, Grammar	■ emphasis on academic interests ■ this emphasis can be to the detriment of pastoral concerns ■ ■	

Phase of education	Features of a teacher in this phase	Implications for the middle manager
Secondary	■ full range of social issues ■ emphasis on raising standards ■ culture of comprehensive education has been challenged considerably ■ links with other phases vary ■ ■	
Special	■ learning programmes are specialised and focused on individuals ■ teaching skills may be valued above subject specialism	
Further Education	■ students may have rejected Secondary education in favour of a tertiary system. In some areas, all post 16 education is tertiary ■ contracts on individual staff will vary ■ opportunities for team work can be limited ■ focus can be on examination results with little notion of pastoral care ■ ■	

In seeking to address these notions of what it means to be a professional in a particular phase, the implications for the middle manager have to be considered. For some they represent constraints on the role the middle manager has, for others there is an opportunity to challenge norms.

 Motivation

Having considered what it is to be a professional in the world of education as a whole and in a particular sphere, the next task is to consider why a teacher wants to be a middle manager. The motivation for the role is important and will certainly be a major factor in determining the success of both an application and the postholder in themselves.

TASK 7

Identifying your motivation

Consider the various motives for seeking promotion set out in Table 2.4.

- In what sense do they apply to you?

- Do you consider these desirable motives?

- How can you show that you possess these motives?

TABLE 2.4 Motives for seeking promotion

Motive	Why is this a desirable motive?	How can you demonstrate this as a motive in a positive manner?	Does this motive apply to you?
Money – you may want/need to earn more.			
Power – you may want to have the power to change or the desire to direct.			
Responsibility			
Frustration			
Personal motivation			
Part of a career plan			
Opportunity			
You have been encouraged to do so.			
Desire to change things			

For some teachers economic necessity is a strong motivation for seeking promotion: rarely, however, is it the sole reason for applying for a promoted post. The reason is not just that the financial reward is not that great, but that which motivates most teachers is the desire to do their best for the pupils in their charge. However, whilst the individual teacher may be able to exert influence over those in their charge, the motivation for seeking promotion is a desire to extend this sphere of influence over a wider group.

The issue of power is a significant one. The power a middle manager is able wield over a group varies considerably – it depends a good deal on the hierarchical structure of the school. In Table 2.5 we raise a number of issues relating to the responsibilities different middle management posts carry with them and the implications for the postholder.

TABLE 2.5 Middle management posts: responsibilities and implications

Post	Examples of responsibilities	Implications for the postholder
Head of Department	■ Will have line responsibility for staff and decide their deployment. ■ Will be involved in recruitment of staff. ■ Will have budget responsibility. ■ Will appraise staff.	■ The postholder needs to consider the nature of management. ■ The postholder needs to clarify his/her staffing policies and plan accordingly. ■ The postholder will need to develop systems for monitoring expenditure and accounting for monies spent. ■ Appraisal is becoming more closely linked to pay and the postholder will need to consider his/her processes with care.
	■ Will be seen as a senior member of staff. ■ As a group, Heads of Departments will be responsible for majority of the curriculum.	■ As a Head of Department, there will be opportunities for collaboration – but there has been a tendency in some organisations for Heads of Departments to compete against one another.

Post	Examples of responsibilities	Implications for the postholder
Subject coordinator in a primary school	■ Will have the responsibility for the development of the subject. ■ For a core subject or National initiative (such as Literacy and Numeracy) the role will have a high profile.	■ There may not be parity in the treatment of subject areas. ■ The role relies on coordinating skills.
Year leader	■ Will recommend the disciplinary sanctions applied to pupils. ■ Will make decisions about pupils. ■ Year Heads operating in cohort will often be a powerful group.	■ The authority is over pupils rather than staff. ■ There may be difficulties in the interface between the pastoral and academic traditions.
Cross-curricular coordinator	■ Nature of cross-curricular initiatives will often receive significant senior management support.	■ The cross-curricular coordinator will need strong organisational skills and the ability to enthuse.
Head of Section (in Further Education (FE))	■ May have to draw up contracts with teachers. ■ Head of Section will have line management responsibility.	■ The postholder may spend a significant amount of time involved in contractual negotiations. In some cases the postholder will have little influence over the contracts and this may weaken his/her status in the organisation. ■ Issues of communication are brought to the fore when managing part-time staff.

Post	Examples of responsibilities	Implications for the postholder
	■ May be the only contact with the hierarchical structures (particularly the part-time lecturers, paid on an hourly basis).	■ In some FE establishments there is a lecture programme which is delivered in the evening – this may affect the control the postholder is able to exert.

However, if we take a more enlightened view of power it is the power to change things for the better. It is about managing a team to bring about change and to improve the quality of education. This is a personal motivation.

Frustration

In some cases the motivation for seeking a middle management role may be some frustration. This frustration may arise from observing problematic features of the educational experience. These features can include:

1 *Philosophical issues* – perhaps it is school policy to teach in sets and the teacher believes in the benefits of mixed ability teaching. The school (or team) may have chosen a particular course and the teacher does not fully support the programme.

2 *Pedagogical issues* – the teaching culture of the school or team may be at variance with the teacher's views. This can be a source of frustration.

3 *Desire to progress in the profession* – the teacher may simply want to be the one who leads the team!

Anyone whose motivation is frustration needs to be careful. Whilst it is surely a factor which influences all those who have progressed there has to be a desire to exert influence and a certain level of disquiet. However, the prospective middle manager needs to be wary of exchanging one set of frustrations for another. Also, if the frustration is in any sense a negative one, this can be detrimental to the recruiting process.

Opportunity

For some middle managers, promotion comes from opportunity. A Year Head may leave unexpectedly, there may be a National initiative, the Head of Department may offer opportunities to a teacher – these are examples where the teacher has the chance to prove worthy of the post. The opportunity to be the 'Acting.....' is one which offers considerable scope for advancement. Many of us have sought promotion because of the encouragement we have been given from our colleagues. This may come from one's Head of Department, a Deputy Headteacher or Headteacher. Indeed, it is an enlightened manager who takes the task of staff development with sufficient seriousness to recommend that a teacher seeks promotion. However, it is part of the profession's responsibility to itself, to develop the skills and attributes in order to facilitate this progression.

For many teachers, however, there is a strong desire to improve the lot of pupils and to increase the opportunities available to them. In some cases we may have witnessed inequality or unfairness. For some of us, there is a recognition that we owe the quality of our lives to the educational opportunities we have been offered. There has to be an element of this in all teachers if they are to succeed and if they are to unlock the potential that exists in the pupils they teach.

However, the mission of the teacher and, in this context, the middle manager, should not be abused. It needs to be acknowledged and valued by school leaders and Government. Too often, teachers work tirelessly to improve and create opportunities and their service goes unrecognised. Many teachers will and do work hard and the remuneration offered does not match either the effort or the result. The altruism of teachers cannot be overstated and is a challenge for all those in management roles in schools. Middle managers should not only recognise this in themselves but also acknowledge this in others. You will need to consider this carefully when preparing to make an application and further, when taking on a middle management post.

Information sources

The main source of information about job vacancies is, of course, *The Times Educational Supplement*. The Jobs section is classified and includes the following categories:

- Nursery
- Infant
- Junior
- Middle
- Secondary
- Special
- Independent

- Local Authority
- Higher Education
- Overseas
- Miscellaneous.

The quality of advertisements does vary but most contain the following information:

1 Name and address of the school.

2 Title of the post and the allowance paid. If this is not specified either by category or in the notice, it needs to be clarified.

3 Brief details about the school and the post and how to apply.

In many cases the school's fax number and increasingly, e-mail and website details will be included. It is useful to visit the website because it gives a valuable insight into how the school operates. The mere existence of a website is an indicator of the school's attitude towards ICT (information and communications technology). Some of the better school websites include the following areas:

1 The recent Ofsted report.

2 Recent examination results.

3 A homepage for parents.

4 The Headteacher's personal e-mail address.

5 An area written by students.

6 The school prospectus.

There are some schools who will not send out information to candidates if it is published on the website. As well as being a means of saving money, it is a way of deselecting those people who do not access the Web.

Most advertisements will invite candidates to send for further details and outline the application procedure. An application pack will comprise some of the following elements:

- About the school – this may include the school prospectus.
- About the job – this may include a person specification and a job specification.
- Details about the Departments (if it is a Subject post).
- Details about the pastoral system.
- An application form.
- Details such as the closing date, interview dates, etc.

_____ Planning an application _____

In this section we are going to consider the following:

1 How to analyse the information available to you.

2 How to read the person specification.

3 How to read the job specification.

4 Writing a letter of application and completing an application form.

5 Writing a curriculum vitae (CV).

6 Sending the covering letter.

7 Interview preparation and etiquette.

8 Questions to consider.

9 Accepting the post.

1. How to analyse the information available to you

Any candidate for a teaching post in a school will need to know basic information about the school and ask some questions about the job they are considering. This section includes a basic proforma to help you analyse the information. Add any other issues in the spaces provided.

TASK 8

Analysing information on a school

Consider the facts about the school and analyse the information.

Think about what the implications would be for you in your current role and school.

Think about how you will demonstrate your preparation for this post with your background.

TABLE 2.6	School information analysis proforma		
Information	**Current school**	**Prospective school**	**Issues to consider**
About the school roll			■ Does a bigger/smaller school fit in with your career plan?
			■ Is the school split-site?
			■ Is the roll stable or rising or falling?
			■ Does the school have enough space for its roll?
			■ Are the buildings adequate?
			■ Are there any funding issues you can identify?
			■
			■
			■
About the headteacher			■ How long has the headteacher been at the school?
			■ What is his/her subject?
			■ Will your teaching subject be an issue in the selection process? (In some cases a range of subjects is necessary to achieve balance in a small team.)
			■
			■
			■
Community information			■ Does the school have links with the local community?
			■ Is the school a community school?

Information	Current school	Prospective school	Issues to consider
			■ Does the community use the school's facilities? (For example, a leisure centre may be on the school campus and the Sports Department may have access to this during the day.)
			■ Is there information about post 16, post 18 relations?
			■ Is there information about the feeder schools?
			■
			■
			■
			■
			■
Links with parents			■ Is there a Parent-Teacher group? This may be an issue for a pastoral role.
			■ Is there a family room?
			■ Do parents act as learning supporters?
			■ Are there home-school contracts?
			■
			■
			■
			■
			■

Information	Current school	Prospective school	Issues to consider
About the staff			■ Are there details about the profile of the staff you can deduce? ■ How many staff are there? ■ How many staff would you line manage? ■ What is the gender profile of the staff? ■ ■
Facilities			■ There are a number of facilities to consider: sports facilities, outdoor areas, hall areas, ICT facilities, open plan schools, etc. ■ ■
Ofsted report			■ How did the school perform? Is it a good school, a very good school, etc.? ■ How did the department you are applying for fare in the report? ■ What are the major issues for the school as a whole? ■ What are the major issues for the department or area of responsibility? ■ ■

Information	Current school	Prospective school	Issues to consider
Prospectus			■ Assess the quality of the prospectus – has it been produced 'in house' or commercially? ■ What information is in the prospectus? ■ Do the pupils look happy? ■ What details are published in the prospectus? ■ ■ ■
Examination results			■ Is the school successful? ■ Is the subject area successful? Are the results in line with other subject areas? ■ How much progress has the school made over recent years? Is it progressing or static? ■ Are there issues you can deduce from the statistics? ■ ■ ■ ■

The first thing to consider is the size of the school. If you are currently teaching in a small school and the post is in a much larger one, you will need to think about how to show that you are aware of the challenges you will face. The team with which you will work may be larger or smaller and there will be interpersonal skills to consider.

The main question to ask at this stage is whether the profile of the school makes you want to work there. Does this seem a place that you could work? If it is important to you to work as part of a close team where you know each other well, then a large team of 12 people may not be the one for you.

However, you need to take care when analysing these documents – there may be issues which may not have been tackled in the material. Some schools take their publicity very seriously and there are some indicators to consider.

TABLE 2.7 Information indicators

Indicator	Possible reasons	Issue for applicant
Paucity of information	■ Some very successful schools do not consider it important to promote themselves. Such a school may have a view that teachers will want to work there because it is what it is. ■ There is no one who can collate the material. This may be the case in a small school or one where there has been a reduction in teaching staff.	■ Is the lack of a prospectus a major issue for you? ■ Do you consider publicity important – could you improve it if you joined that school? ■ Are there funding issues?
Information is inaccurate or incomplete.	■ The school may be in difficulties and so may choose to give very brief details. ■ In the case of a failing school, the quality of information itself may be an issue.	■ The challenge of a failing or struggling school is considerable and the candidate needs to consider how the middle manager will address it. ■ The school may have made a lot of progress but there has not been opportunity to review

Indicator	Possible reasons	Issue for applicant
		promotional materials. It is worthwhile being charitable; otherwise an opportunity may be lost.
Details about the post are vague. The allowance to be paid may not be stated.	■ Some posts may be subject to change or be ones which evolve, e.g. a cross-curricular role. ■ The school may be undergoing considerable change. ■ The school may have budget constraints which are unresolved. ■ There can be flexibility because of the nature of the post. If a candidate has certain skills then the post can be organised around them.	■ The details of the remuneration should be clear. It is important to clarify the details. ■ The candidate's individual profile may give considerable flexibility.

2. How to read the person specification

There is a growing practice in any appointment procedure to include a person specification. Such a specification will normally be in two sections – essential attributes and desirable attributes.

The essential part of the specification means that without all the attributes listed you will not be considered further for the post. However, posts which are difficult to fill may be prepared to waive some essential criteria. The person specification needs to be read carefully. You must ensure when applying that you demonstrate all the essential elements and as many of the desirable criteria as possible.

In each case the criteria will be assessed by either:

■ letter of application

■ reference

■ curriculum vitae

■ interview process.

TASK 9

Responding to a person specification

Read the following person specification and decide how the selection panel will assess whether the candidate meets the criteria, e.g. by CV, interview, references or letter of application.

TABLE 2.8 Person specification for Head of Modern Languages

Criteria	Essential	Desirable	Assessed by
Qualifications	■ First degree in Modern Foreign Language (MFL) ■ Speaks more than one language	■ Higher degree in MFL ■ Qualified to at least 'A' Level in second language	
Experience	■ Taught first language for at least ten years ■ Evidence of successful teaching to 'A' Level ■ Evidence of successful project management ■ Evidence of wider curriculum involvement	■ Taught more than one language ■ Taught in more than one school ■ Has taught second language to at least GCSE level ■ Experienced at managing change	
Personal attributes	■ Commitment ■ Integrity ■ Adaptability to changing circumstances and new ideas ■ Sense of humour		

Criteria	Essential	Desirable	Assessed by
Skills and competencies	■ ICT capability ■ Can plan, prioritise and organise ■ Can demonstrate high-level organisational skills ■ Excellent classroom practitioner ■ Clear written and spoken communication	■ Evidence of interest in curriculum development ■ A commitment to promoting high quality teaching and evidence of having raised standards	

3. How to read the job specification

The job specification is about the broader details of the job. It specifies the tasks for which the responsibility is given. It will include a range of managerial and leadership functions.

TASK 10

Responding to a job description

Many schools are using the National Standards for Subject Leaders to devise their job descriptions and this task challenges you to consider how you would respond to this job description.

TABLE 2.9 A middle manager's job description

Job description for a middle manager	Your response
Strategic direction and development 1. To develop and implement policies and practices for the subject which reflect the school's commitment to high achievement, effective teaching and learning.	

Job description for a middle manager	Your response

2. To create a climate which enables other staff to develop and maintain both positive attitudes towards the subject and confidence in teaching it.

3. Use data effectively to identify pupils who are underachieving in the subject and, where necessary, create and implement effective plans of actions to support those pupils.

Teaching and learning

1. Ensure curriculum coverage, continuity and progression in the subject for all pupils.

2. Ensure that teachers are clear about the teaching objectives in lessons, understand the sequence of teaching and learning in the subject, and communicate such information to pupils.

3. Provide guidance on the choice of appropriate teaching and learning methods.

4. Establish and implement clear policies and practices for assessing, recording and reporting on pupil achievement.

Leading and managing staff

1. Help staff to achieve constructive working relationships with pupils.

2. Establish clear expectations and constructive working relationships among staff involved with the subject, including through team working and mutual support; devolving responsibilities and delegating tasks.

3. Sustain your own motivation, and where possible, that of other staff.

4. Appraise staff as required.

Job description for a middle manager	Your response
5. Ensure that the headteacher, senior managers and governors are well informed about subject policies, plans and priorities, the success in meeting objectives and targets and subject-related professional development plans.	
Efficient and effective deployment of staff and resources	
1. Establish staff and resource needs for the subject and advise the headteacher and senior managers of likely priorities.	
2. Deploy staff, or advise the headteacher on the deployment of staff.	
3. Ensure the effective and efficient management and organisation of learning resources.	
4. Ensure that there is a safe working and learning environment in which risks are properly assessed.	

The objective of this exercise is not that the middle manager should demonstrate that he/she can do all of the tasks but that the middle manager can demonstrate the competencies required. One way in which the middle manager can do this both in the letter of application and in the interview process, is to describe an initiative where he/she has demonstrated expertise in these areas and which shows that he/she has ideas on how these areas might be tackled.

The recruitment process for a middle manager is crucial to the success of a school. The headteacher has to assess, using the application, the references and the interview data, whether the candidate has the ability to do the job. Not only is a teacher being recruited, but also a manager.

4. Writing a letter of application and completing an application form

Writing a letter of application for a job is more difficult than completing an application form because there is no structure to the task.

The main points about application forms are obvious ones, but it is surprising how many worthy candidates prejudice their applications by a failure to act on them.

TABLE 2.10 Points to remember when completing an application form

- Answer all the questions. If a question is not applicable, write N/A next to it.
- Write or type in black – your application will be photocopied for the interview process.
- List your qualifications in chronological order.
- Emphasise any qualifications specified in the person description.
- Use any space which asks for details of recent training to illustrate your preparation for the job.
- Include your degree class and 'A' Level grades. GCSE and 'O' Levels are less relevant, but may be required.
- There is normally a space asking about hobbies and interests – include details which demonstrate your personal qualities.
- Absence record – this is becoming increasingly common and it is important to quote this accurately as it will normally be included as part of a reference.
- Criminal record – be honest, even about speeding fines, as an application may not proceed without accurate police checks.
- Referees – include the name, title, postal address, telephone and fax numbers.
- Use the space for the letter of application on the form as indicated. Set out the letter as if you were writing a formal letter.
- Make sure that you follow the application procedure exactly and that you include all the details requested.

Writing a letter is in some ways more difficult, but it does give you the opportunity to explain why you should be considered. Having used the information to analyse the school, it is important that your letter shows that you have considered the strengths and weaknesses of the school and the post for which you are applying. Your letter should cover the following points:

- relevant experience
- successful management of change
- management training undertaken

- achievements in teaching and learning – it is worthwhile including your classes' exam results, where appropriate

- extra curricular involvement.

One way to construct such a letter is to 'brainstorm' all the points to be included in the letter. The letter could follow the template shown in Table 2.11.

TABLE 2.11 Application letter model

1 What you do currently and what job you are applying to do.

2 What your current role is and how this has prepared you for the job.

3 Why you want to do the job at this school.

4 Your philosophy of teaching the subject (or teaching in general).

5 Your interest in the subject.

6 Your involvement in the wider life of the school.

- Sometimes you may be asked to describe, for example, a change you managed or a problem you resolved – the application must fulfil all that is requested.

- The letter should be no more that two sides of A4 in a readable font.

- The letter should be enthusiastic in tone.

- The letter should be individual and convey the person who is applying for the job.

The task which follows focuses on the essential parts of a letter of application.

TASK 11

Analysing a letter of application

Read the letter of application in Table 2.12 below for the position of Head of Mathematics.

Identify the ways in which the candidate explains why she wants the job and how she details her skills.

TABLE 2.12 An example of a letter of application

8 Boulter Drive
Buckland
Oxon.
OX4 1JG
10th March, 2000

Mr C. Cohen
Headmaster
Mannion School
The Green
Mannion
Devon.

Dear Mr Cohen,

I am an experienced teacher seeking a management appointment. I am particularly looking for a position which involves curriculum organisation and personnel management and believe that your advertised post for the **Head of Mathematics** may offer the career development I seek.

In my career so far I have undertaken a range of academic and organisational aspects of secondary education, preparing students for the syllabuses of several examination boards and Oxbridge. My own involvement in public examinations has given me a particular confidence in interpreting assessment objectives and creating learning opportunities for young people of various ages and abilities. As a former Head of Department I am familiar with the day-to-day business of a busy department and the management of both specialist and non-specialist staff at varying stages in their careers. I am used to presenting the work of a department and a school to colleagues, parents and other agencies.

I am currently studying for an M.A. in Education Management. This course has proved to be useful in both personal and professional terms. I have had the opportunity to analyse and review my theories of school management in the light of further study and interaction with prominent theorists in the field. Also, learning about the development of the school budget and its relationship with the school development plan has proved instructive and informative.

My strengths as a mathematician are in the areas of Pure Mathematics and Mechanics and as a member of a wider staff team, in my willingness to adapt, collaborate and take responsibility for initiatives. I would like this post to give me scope to use and develop these skills.

The past few years have seen a number of changes in the teaching profession and I consider the priorities at this time to be the maintenance of the status of knowledge in terms of access to further and higher education and as a curriculum-wide preparation for adult life. I believe that education, in its broadest sense, has to provide a disciplined academic method which is transferable and a benefit to young people's development as thinking and responsible citizens. For example, the ability to research, to analyse and to generalise are all features of my Mathematics teaching and underpin my philosophy of Mathematics teaching.

The creativity of the teaching profession and individual teachers' ability to create exciting learning opportunities are two of the vitally important elements of our education system. We shall need to continue to develop our curriculum and ensure that the emerging system represents the best for our pupils and includes opportunities to use teachers' considerable knowledge and skills.

In my current post we have developed a home-school learning initiative where parents regularly test their children on Mental Mathematics. I have led this project and we have measured a significant improvement in the recall of tables by the children in Year 7.

I would want to build for success. This success will be achieved with the hard work of the students and the staff. I would want to develop a scheme of work which encompasses the best traditions with the needs of the future. I would want to develop the SMP scheme that you currently use and look for ways of enriching the scheme, so that lessons are fully differentiated and so that students enjoy success at all stages of their Mathematics education. I see an evaluation of A Level courses being an important step. Also, I would want to make full use of computers and graphical calculators throughout the school as part of a modern investigative approach which has its roots in rigour and disciplined academic method.

If I have learnt anything from my brief career break and my gradual return to full-time teaching, albeit on a temporary contract, it is that learning is not always divisible by lesson bells, subject differences or assumptions about expectable Key Stage Attainment. Rather it is a complex matter of motivation and gender and social experience with implications in the variety of access through task and purpose. This view has a particular impact on the way in which I plan both schemes of work and individual lessons. I plan an area of work as an integrated whole, i.e. through practical activities, problem solving and investigations. All students then can generalise and then benefit fully from consolidation. Essentially, teaching and learning take place in a context.

I enjoy school life and working with students and their teachers tremendously. As a teacher, I have always been fully involved in the life of the school. It is sometimes difficult to find time for extra activities but I regularly take Assembly, I sing with the school choir and I run a lunchtime Aerobics Club.

If appointed I would seek to demonstrate energy, good-humoured efficiency and a strong commitment to the highest standards of ambition and good behaviour.

Yours sincerely

This letter would be successful for the following reasons:

1 It sets out the key elements of the position being applied for and the reason why the applicant wants to do the job.

2 The applicant explains how he/she will be able to do the functional aspects of the job

3 The applicant identifies his/her strengths as a classroom practitioner.

4 The applicant describes briefly a project he/she has led and highlights the evaluation that has been done.

5 The applicant explains how he/she will manage the change from the existing scheme of work to incorporate new ideas. The applicant shows that he/she has researched the school and has thought how he/she can operate within it.

6 The applicant conveys an enthusiasm not only for the job, but also for school life in general.

5. Writing a curriculum vitae (CV)

A CV is not always required because of the use of an application form. However, over recent years schools have moved away from relying on an application form to seeking a letter plus CV. There are several reasons for this change. One reason is to save money – the school does not have to print application forms or spend money posting them to any applicants. Also, when schools moved from local authority control, it became a symbol of their independence to be able to break away from the 'mould' of the application form. There was also a realisation that to get the fullest picture of an applicant a less restrictive process was needed.

Personal computers make producing a CV comparatively straightforward. There are even packages designed to help you construct one. There is no set order for a CV but it should contain the following information as a matter of course:

TABLE 2.13 A model CV

1 Personal details – name, address, telephone, e-mail, NI number, teacher's number

2 Current post – the title and main responsibilities

3 Recent courses and professional development

4 Recent projects and initiatives

5 Qualifications – Degree, 'A' Levels, etc.

6 Teaching history

7 Referees

There are other headings that might be included such as hobbies and interests, employment outside teaching, etc. The headings are a personal choice. The CV needs to be regularly updated and can easily be tailored to the demands of a particular application.

6. Sending the covering letter

A covering letter should be used when there is an application form only. It should be addressed to the headteacher and state that you are applying for the named post and that you include an application form.

Such a letter is important not only because of the etiquette but also because it enables a busy headteacher to focus on the purpose of your letter. In a large school, it is not unusual for there to be up to 20 teaching posts vacant each year.

Popular schools can attract up to a hundred applications for a promoted post and anything which makes the task straightforward for the school will be welcomed.

7. Interview preparation and etiquette

The timetable for the selection day will vary from school to school but will include some of the following events. Table 2.14 also provides notes and comments on each event.

TABLE 2.14 Selection day events with notes and comments

Event	Notes	Comments
Introduction by the headteacher	■ This is so that the headteacher can meet the candidates and tell them a little about the school and the programme for the day. ■ This meeting rarely forms part of the selection procedure.	■ Usually a very pleasant part of the day. ■ There may be the opportunity for questions but you should not try to over-impress with big questions. ■ Dress appropriately; this is the first impression you will make.
Tour of the school – often by pupils	■ This gives candidates an insight into the school at work. ■ Pupils may be asked for feedback on how candidates responded. ■ This is to see if you are observant.	■ A possible question at interview is to comment on something you have observed whilst on the tour.
Visit to the Department/ faculty/team area	■ How do you relate to members of the team? ■ What do you ask to see? ■ What questions do you ask? ■ What information do you find out?	■ This may include a talk with the present incumbent.

Event	Notes	Comments
Making a presentation	You will be tested on: ■ Presenting your ideas to an audience ■ Personal presence ■ Doing a presentation to time ■ Response to questions from the audience.	■ Try to inspect the venue beforehand. ■ Check to see if you can use an OHP or flip-chart. ■ If appropriate, produce handouts – but distribute at the end of the presentation. ■ Answer the audience, not only the person asking the question.
You may be asked to teach a lesson	■ Your skill as a classroom practitioner will be under scrutiny	■ Show what you can do. Show how you enjoy teaching your subject. Show that you like teaching children. ■ Consider the Ofsted criteria for a successful lesson – schools will often invite the subject adviser or the Link adviser to assist them in the selection process.
Lunch	■ Usually with staff, but may be in the school cafeteria. In primary schools and special schools lunch will usually be with the children. ■ This is to see how you behave out of class.	■ It is important to appreciate that you are on show all of the time. ■ In some schools, anyone who comes into contact with a candidate gives feedback to the panel. This can include lunchtime supervisors, crossing patrol staff, etc.

8. Questions to consider

The purpose of the interview is to assess whether you are the right person for the school. Having written a successful letter which has been supported by your referee, the interview is the main method for selecting the successful applicant. There are a number of general points to consider before we discuss the questions normally asked:

- use names
- answer the question concisely
- do not rush into an answer – pause for thought. The time you spend thinking may seem an age to you, but you will give a considered answer as a result
- give examples based on your experience
- try to pick up on things you have learnt about the school
- conclude the answer and then stop.

The questions asked at an interview for a middle management position are designed to test your ability to lead and manage a team.

TASK 12

Interview questions

Read the questions in Table 2.15.

Write three bullet points to make each response.

Which criteria from the person specification and job description does each question test?

TABLE 2.15 Interview questions

Question	Response	Criteria from person and job descriptions
Why should pupils learn your subject?		
What are the strengths/weaknesses of the subject team?		

Question	Response	Criteria from person and job descriptions
What strategies do you have for improving results at Key Stage X?		
You are appointed today; in a year's time how would you know if you had done a good job?		
What do you look for in a successful lesson?		
How would you assert your authority?		
How would you support a member of the team who teaches disruptive pupils?		
When monitoring the marking of your team, you discover one teacher has not marked the books for a term. What would you do?		
You receive a complaint from a parent about a teacher in your team. The parent says the teacher has lost the GCSE coursework. The teacher says he gave it back to the pupil. What do you do?		

9. Accepting the post

Some schools do not notify candidates of the results of their application until the successful applicant has been offered the post. Other schools phone people with the result very quickly. The offer is a firm contract, although it may be subject to police checks and the like. Therefore, in accepting the job, you are accepting the contract.

It is a great feeling to be given the job you have striven for. The challenges are now firmly ahead of you, but you can be secure in your knowledge that you have thought carefully about the issues underpinning the role. You can be pleased with your appointment because, in making your application in the manner described in this chapter, the school has appointed you for your strengths. You need to be honest in any application – it is bad advice to try to be what they want – it is always better to be yourself. In that way, everyone can be secure in the decision they have made.

Summary

At the end of this chapter it is our intention that you will:

- have considered the core purpose of a subject leader
- have a perspective on the function of education, the nature of educational provision and what it means to be a professional teacher
- have considered your motives for wanting promotion
- know the ways in which you can find out about promoted posts
- be able to analyse the information about a school and in particular, the person and job specifications
- create a job application – including a CV and letter of application
- prepare for an interview for a middle management post.

chapter three

Starting out

Appointment

Visiting the new school

Getting to know everyone

Setting the agenda for the
first few months

Taking care of yourself

Leading change

Time management

Summary

T his chapter is called *Starting Out* because it deals with the first few weeks and months of being a middle manager. There is likely to be a very steep learning curve and this chapter is designed to help the newly appointed middle manager to take those important first steps.

This chapter is divided into several sections which deal with:

- initial actions on being appointed
- making the first visit to the school after appointment
- the first team meeting
- the first few days in the new role
- dealing with a member of the team who also applied for the job
- setting the agenda for the first few months
- dealing with stress
- leading strategic change – the change process
- day-to-day administration and procedures.

Appointment

In the previous chapter we discussed the application and interview process and we stressed the importance articulating honestly your views and opinions. This will now become of real importance. The application process is designed to enable the headteacher and Governors to decide which of the candidates is right to lead the team. By appointing somebody they are demonstrating their confidence in that person.

In the previous chapter we emphasised the need to be yourself at the interview and to ensure that the opinions you gave were your own and not an attempt to second guess the school's own agenda. When considering the first few months of the job, it is important to refer back to the principles you articulated in the appointment process.

Securing a middle management post is a cause for celebration. A middle manager has great influence in the development of the subject or the welfare of the pastoral team or indeed the section of the school under charge. The responsibility is great but there are those whose support you can engage and the task becomes less onerous. After the celebrations are over, there is for most, a time when the question arises 'What have I done?' For a teacher this is perhaps, more of an issue than for other occupations. School life can be all consuming and it is likely that you will have to leave the school in which you are already a strong and successful teacher so that you can take up a promotion. Good teachers enjoy working with the pupils in their care; many teachers become fond of their pupils and have a close relationship with them. It is not easy to walk away from a group of children who like you, enjoy working for you and with you and to step out into the unknown, to an alien environment where everyone knows everyone except for you. This may be overstating the case, but there is for all teachers some element of regret when leaving a school. The rhythm of the school year and the nature of the appointment process means that you will have been at the school you are leaving for some time – perhaps a number of years. The stress of this change needs to be acknowledged.

However, you have new challenges ahead and once you have come to terms with leaving the school, you must turn your attention to the new organisation. It is important to disengage from the current school in order to focus on the new role. This process happens naturally as the time comes to an end. Telling children that you are leaving is an important step. However, it is worth taking the advice of senior staff as to when children are told. The following sequence is useful to consider:

TABLE 3.1 Actions on being appointed

1. Inform the headteacher of your success.

2. Inform your current line manager of your success – the rest of the staff will hear via the staffroom grapevine!

3. Write to your referees telling them of your success and thanking them for writing a reference.

4. You should receive the offer in writing and write your reply. You can then write a letter of resignation.

5. Arrange a visit to your new school to prepare for the new job.

6. If you are involved in any projects where you liaise with other schools, it is important to inform these people of your impending departure.

7 Decide with your line manager when your classes will be told – it may be worth waiting until your successor is appointed. Then you can say 'At the end of this term I am leaving the school and you will be taught by Mr X'.

This sequence of events is important because your colleagues will remember you in a more favourable light if you observe these niceties. Further, in the future, you may wish to apply to the school for a reference or even for another post at that school. More importantly, however, it is about adopting a professional stance and acting correctly and with propriety. For the children in the class, the prospect of a new teacher can bring about feelings of insecurity. This is particularly the case for those who are preparing for public examinations. To be able to say whom the new teacher will be demonstrates your lasting commitment to them and shows your control over the situation. In some cases, however, there may be disciplinary difficulties if children believe that their teacher is leaving. There is no easy answer to this problem – children are surprisingly clever at finding out this sort of thing. They are adept at overhearing conversations – and then rumours begin. You are then in a difficult position – should you deny the rumours? It is always ill advised to lie to children – the trust that exists, of necessity, between a teacher and child is easily lost in the face of an obvious untruth.

Having told classes of your departure, your best defence is to carry on as normal. It is important to maintain the standards of discipline, to continue as if you were staying. This will maintain the quality of relationships and avoid any difficulties. Further, you still have the responsibility for the class and it is your professional responsibility to maintain standards. Where the appointment is for a September start there may be period of several months before you take up the post.

Continuing to work hard with classes and behaving 'as normal', will, in many cases, put the fact that the teacher is leaving out of the children's minds. Further, in settling matters at school, you are ensuring that your classes are passed to the new teacher with the minimum of disruption to the children's education. This is professional responsibility.

—————— Visiting the new school ——————

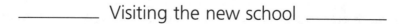

Having begun the process of disengaging from the school and preparing for the new role, you need to arrange a visit to the new school. For the most part, schools will release a teacher for at least a day. However, if more time is required, the new school may be asked to pay for supply costs to cover the absence. It is important to negotiate these details with the headteachers to facilitate a smooth transition and minimise any disquiet. The visit to the new school will be important because it will be your first chance to meet the team and start to learn about the job that you will be doing. There are several tasks which you need to undertake before visiting the new school.

Preparing for a meeting with the headteacher

This will be the first meeting with the headteacher since your appointment and it is important that you make a positive impression. The headteacher will want to be sure that you have made the right choice in accepting the appointment. By presenting yourself as well organised and focused on the task ahead, you will make good progress in maintaining the positive impression.

TASK 13

Preparing for initial meetings 1

This task is designed to help you to plan for meeting with the headteacher and constructing an agenda for the meeting.

You are preparing to visit your new school and you will be having a short meeting with the headteacher. There is no agenda for this 30-minute meeting.

Using Table 3.2 write in the reasons why it is important to address the considerations identified.

TABLE 3.2 The importance of preparing for initial meetings

Agenda	Considerations	Why is this important at this stage?
Preparing an agenda for the short meeting	■ Demonstrates a well-organised approach ■ Demonstrates commitment ■ Sets the tone for a purposeful meeting ■ Allows you to exert some control over what is discussed ■ The control element will help to settle any nervousness	

Agenda	Considerations	Why is this important at this stage?
First priorities – the meeting with the team later on	■ By articulating your intentions for the team meeting this will add to the headteacher's positive view ■ By articulating your agenda the headteacher can offer guidance and support ■ It gives the headteacher the opportunity to 'fill you in' on any developments since your appointment ■ There may be staffing issues of which you were unaware and the headteacher has the opportunity to explain these to you	
Your priorities for the first few weeks	■ It is important not to set yourself a programme that is overly ambitious ■ The balance needs to be struck between doing very little and trying to do too much – the headteacher can offer guidance on your priorities ■ It is important not to worry if the headteacher makes other suggestions – he/she knows the school and is giving you the benefit of his/her direction	

Agenda	Considerations	Why is this important at this stage?
Arrangements for a subsequent meeting	■ This is a proactive middle manager. Stance will demonstrate a strong leadership trait and will pay dividends in the future	

The objectives of this meeting are to begin the induction process and to engage support. By articulating your priorities for the first few weeks, you are confirming the wisdom of your appointment. It is vital for the future success of the team that such an initial meeting is planned. You may be concerned. The headteacher will normally wish to guide you and want to offer advice and support. This is particularly important when leading a team where there have been difficulties. For the new middle manager, it is crucial that you consider very carefully what advice you are offered – only a very confident person neglects the guidance!

You need to have considered carefully your priorities for those first few weeks. There is something of a dilemma to be faced here. At the start of a new job, you are likely to be bursting with ideas and full of enthusiasm – this is certainly desirable, if not essential. There will, of course, be a measure of nervousness and anxiety at the prospect of the fresh challenge. The balance that has to be struck is between trying to achieve too much in the first weeks and failing to make a positive impression. You have been appointed because of your ideas and the belief that you have the skills to lead the team to higher standards of achievement. However, a team takes time to build and there is opportunity to achieve goals but in a planned and measured manner.

Your first priorities will include:

■ learning your way around the school
■ learning the systems of the school
■ establishing yourself with classes
■ getting to know the team
■ beginning to bring about change.

The balance is a difficult one because everyone will be looking towards you to see what you do in the first few weeks. Members of the team will have some anxieties because of the uncertainty that any change brings about. A clear agenda will be useful at this stage.

TASK 14

Preparing for initial meetings 2

This task builds on the scenario used in Task 13 on page 69.

A team meeting is scheduled for the end of the school day on which you are making your initial visit to the school. In the letter arranging the visit it is suggested that you lead this meeting.

Complete Table 3.3 below.

TABLE 3.3 Preparing for the first team meeting

Agenda item	Considerations	Why it is important for the first meeting?
Opening remarks	■ You may have met all of the team at the interview, but they may not remember all that much about you (this is not from disrespect, but it was a working day for them, and they will have met the other candidates too!). ■ By introducing yourself to them you can show yourself to be warm, friendly and professional. ■ You establish the tone for the meeting. ■ You may consider asking each person to introduce himself or herself to you – this will enable you to learn everyone's name. But, a large team may take rather a long time.	

Agenda item	Considerations	Why it is important for the first meeting?
Your philosophy	■ It is worthwhile articulating your philosophy for education and your subject, if appropriate. ■ For a Subject team it is important that the leader has a view on the purpose of the subject. It is important to state this clearly, but if it is at variance with what you have found out about the team, the statement needs to be tempered. ■ This strong statement of your philosophy will set the scene for the work you are to do with the team. ■ It is useful to consider how you state your philosophy – and show the transition from the previous leadership to yours. If this can be done in a manner which is coherent, difficulties can be lessened.	
Your principles	■ At this stage you can state how you will conduct yourself with the team.	

Agenda item	Considerations	Why it is important for the first meeting?
	■ The team needs to know how you will work with them – there may be uncertainties over this and your statement will give direction and help to address insecurities. ■ The balance here is between your role as a middle manager and as a teacher. It is important to appreciate the role and its implications.	
The first project	■ By choosing a project which is small-scale but which involves the whole team, you can establish yourself readily. ■ You should choose a project in which you are confident and which does not depend heavily on the skills of the team, but which provides an opportunity for the team to enjoy success in a joint endeavour. ■ If you have materials already prepared for this section, this will emphasise your organisational capability.	
Time to interact	■ Your team will need to get to know you and a time for interaction is appropriate.	

Having prepared for such a meeting the outcome will be that you have:

- introduced yourself to the team
- started to get to know the team
- articulated your philosophy
- begun the process of managing the team, by stating your principles. These are inviolate statements which you can refer to as time goes on
- emphasised your management capability by setting up a small-scale project which will enable you to work with the team.

You will probably be nervous about the outcome of this meeting. The first meeting with the new group is always a challenge. It may even be the first meeting you have chaired. However, by deciding the format and the outcomes, the challenge will be made easier.

The actual timing of the meeting is relevant here. All schoolteachers are subject to *directed time*. The Teachers' Pay and Conditions Document (TPCD) is published each year by the Secretary of State for Education. This sets out the pay scale and the determining factors to be applied in deciding the point on the scale at which any teacher in a particular post will start. It also sets out in significant detail the conditions of employment, specifying the directed time of 1265 hours per year that a teacher must be available to work under the direction of the headteacher, and the duties that are to be performed both within and outside the directed time. For the most part, meetings of this kind will fall under the directed time aegis. Therefore, the meeting may be specified to last one hour, for example. It is important, therefore, that this meeting does not overrun. It will demonstrate good managerial skill if the meeting is controlled in such a way that the meeting is effectively chaired and sensitively managed to finish on time. Some people like to place their watch in front of them to help them to gauge the time accurately; others will decide, in advance, the amount of time to be spent on a particular item on the agenda and arrange the meeting accordingly. In planning this first meeting, it is worthwhile checking to ascertain if there are any other matters which need to be dealt with during that time. If the meeting only occurs as part of a five- or six-week cycle, then it is likely that there are important procedural and administrative matters to address.

Getting to know everyone

The first few days of the new job are likely to be stressful but also, in our experience, very pleasant. They will be stressful because there is so much with which to become acquainted. Moving from the position where one knows everyone and is fully conversant with all the systems to a place where everything is unfamiliar is very stressful. The learning you have to do is heightened by the need to become established in the new role. However, whilst expectations of you may be high (that is why you have been appointed) there is a recognition that it does take time for people to settle in before they can be at their most effective.

Your priorities in your first few days in the role of middle manager are as follows:

- getting to know the team – their strengths and weaknesses
- getting to know the team as teachers
- establishing yourself with your classes
- getting to know the staff.

Getting to know your team

Your first priority is to learn about the staff in the team. This is vital if the team is to make progress and you are to manage the team effectively. Some managers may wish to have an individual meeting with each member of the team and conduct some sort of fact finding exercise. If there is the time to do this, it can be a very useful and efficient way in which to set the tone for the future workings of the team. If, however, the nature of the school or the team is contrary to this method of working, you will have to decide whether this is the most suitable way of getting to know the team.

TASK 15

Finding out about your team

Using Table 3.4 below, think about the kind of information you need to find out.

Think also about the kind of response you might anticipate from the individual teachers.

Consider how you will respond to hostility or indifference.

If there are particular management issues within the team (for example, incompetence, long-term grievances, etc.) how will you manage these within the context of this interview process?

TABLE 3.4 Finding out about your team

Information required	Considerations	Possible responses	Why is this information important?
How long the teacher has taught at the school.	■ This is useful information because it gives you the profile of the team, by service. ■ You need to be aware that a possible response is 'Too long'.		
How long the teacher has been a teacher.	■ Whilst it is important to be reflective as a teacher, the response can induce some melancholy from those who appear or may be disillusioned. ■ The response to this question may warn you of disquiet or difficulty. This is particularly the case where you have been promoted rapidly.		
What the teacher's academic background is.	■ Some tact and caution may be required here. In the main, teachers		

Information required	Considerations	Possible responses	Why is this information important?
	will happily talk about themselves, but if there is unfulfilled ambition, then the signs will be evident.		
What the range of classes taught this academic year has been.	■ This is useful to ask because most teachers like to talk about their classes. ■ It allows you to ask about specific classes. This is useful if the development required is within a key stage.		
How the teacher responded to Ofsted.	■ If the Ofsted is recent then the teacher will have a grading. The gradings are confidential to the teacher and the headteacher. ■ If you consider the response to this together with the Ofsted report, you can begin to build up a profile of teacher competence.		

Information required	Considerations	Possible responses	Why is this information important?
What the teacher's results for their classes have been over the past three years.	■ Again, many teachers enjoy talking about their classes and asking this will both emphasise the purpose of the meeting and also give the teacher the opportunity to describe their successes or otherwise. ■ The teacher may put forward reasons to explain the results and this is valuable information when planning curriculum change.		
What the teacher sees as the priorities for the team.	■ This needs to be handled carefully. The responses should reveal team's views about the development that has been undertaken before. Each teacher can have their say at the outset.		

Information required	Considerations	Possible responses	Why is this information important?
	■ You need to be careful that you don't make promises you cannot or may not be able to keep. It is vital that you establish yourself as a principled person who undertakes only what they are committed to do.		

Creating a team profile

The agenda for such a meeting could vary considerably from Table 3.4, but these are important questions which need to be answered. The results of these discussions will enable you to compile a profile of the team under the following headings and answer these questions:

TABLE 3.5 Team profile proforma

Question	Profile of the team	Issues for development	Team members who will support development	Team members who will resist development
What is the balance within the team? Gender, experience, time at the school, academic background		■ Are there training needs		
Monitoring of teachers' work		■ Has the experience of inspection been a positive one?		

Question	Profile of the team	Issues for development	Team members who will support development	Team members who will resist development
		■ Have the issues from Ofsted been addressed?		
Are the results for the team in line with expectations?		■ What do teachers expect?		
		■ What use is made of benchmark data?		
What is the team's response to change?		■ Do the team see the need for change?		
		■ Is the change you have planned anticipated?		
Is the team cohesive and coherent? How have the team responded to this fact finding?		■ Is the issue of team building an urgent one?		
		■ How will the team respond to being managed?		
		■ Are there difficulties with the management style adopted at this early stage?		

Having a team profile enables you to decide how to start to lead the team. Of course, this process can be tailored to meet the culture of the school. Schools which are run very much on a business model would welcome this approach. However, a small village school, where the manager is a subject coordinator, may find this approach too radical and any attempt to conduct this kind of interview may be met with strong resistance. The well-meant objective may be scuppered by how people react to the management style. This is a health warning for all managers in schools. The rationale and the process may be absolutely sound, but if the cultural change is too great, the process will not be successful in the long term and the manager's job will be more difficult the next time around.

This issue illustrates the dilemma of school management. Whilst one person is charged with leading a team and bears responsibility for the tasks that are set, successful schools work on the basis of cooperation and a commitment to teamwork. Teachers are not proletarians who can be told to do things in a certain way. Whilst they can be directed to perform certain tasks, subversion (to give it the most pejorative name) is practised to a great extent in schools because of the isolated nature of the teaching process. However, this issue will be discussed in greater depth in Chapter 4.

Getting to know the team as teachers

In order to bring about improvements to the quality of teaching, you will need to have a view on the quality of teaching and learning within the team. Whilst the Ofsted report – where it exists – is a useful source of information, you need to assess this for yourself. You can organise a programme of lesson observation over a period of time and this will have the effect of emphasising your quality control function. Of course, as a new manager, you have a good reason for wanting to undertake this process: simply because you are new. However, in the bid to establish yourself with your own classes, you need to plan the lesson observations with some care.

A useful way to begin the dialogue on the quality of teaching and learning is to establish with the team:

1 That the purpose of lesson observation, at this stage, is for you to gain information about the teaching strengths of the team.

2 That you will make the criteria for the lesson observation clear to all.

3 That you will give feedback from the lesson observation.

4 That, where possible, teachers can choose which class you observe.

The purpose of this procedure is to be open and honest with the team. The teachers may still have anxieties about the new regime and this approach leaves no room for anyone to suggest a hidden agenda for the observations. The criteria for the lesson observation should be clearly stated and should be fairly bland at this stage. Much can be gained by observing the relationship between the teacher and the class.

As an opening strategy, the criteria for these lesson observations could be:

1 The quality of relationships between teacher and pupils.

2 How the teacher introduces the work to the class.

3 How much time is spent on tasks during the lesson.

4 How the tasks are differentiated.

5 The link between class work and homework.

There are a number of other criteria which could be substituted in this list but the objective for the observation needs to be kept in mind. The purpose is to enable you to construct a profile of the teaching in the team. As part of the feedback to the teacher, both you and the teacher could use the following proforma.

TABLE 3.6 Teacher observation feedback proforma

Lesson evaluation	Response
How did you link the lesson with previous and future learning?	
Did you explain and illustrate clearly what you expected pupils to achieve by the end of the lesson?	
How did you communicate your expectations to the pupils?	
Did all the pupils behave appropriately during the lesson? What strategies did you use to ensure this?	
What teaching strategies did you use and how effective were they?	
What questioning techniques did you use?	
What activities did you think were successful in your lesson? What criteria did you use to assess success?	
What work did the pupils produce in the lesson? How will you assess it?	
What homework did you set for this class? How will you assess it?	
If you planned this lesson again, how would you plan it differently?	

The benefits of such a proforma are that, at this stage, the criteria for the evaluation are not particularly contentious and involve the teacher in the act. This is important when establishing a dialogue with the teacher to discuss their work. It is vital, in these early stages, to create a forum where the quality of teaching and learning are discussed in an open and honest way, and that you are seen as proactive and yet supportive. There may be a time when you have to assert yourself and act as a disciplinary agent, but if this process is not to be compromised you should avoid it at this stage.

An additional priority in the first few days is to establish yourself with your classes. You will need to be a highly effective classroom practitioner and you set the standard for the rest of the team. It is part of the management function to set standards and these will be compromised if you are found wanting in any respect. However, you are not a superhero and you need to bear this in mind. Certainly, there are some aspects of the job where there is no compromise on standards. These include:

- preparation for class
- quality of teaching
- quality of assessment and marking
- consistency of behaviour management.

However, this is not to say that you will never get things wrong. Every leader needs to have a measure of humility and be prepared to own up to both the enormity of the task and the impossibility of perfection; however, you cannot be found wanting when the issues concern the standards of teaching and learning. This is the professional manager.

You can use your interactions with your own classes to establish yourself in the school. By focusing on the quality of teaching and learning and demonstrating effective and consistent behaviour management, the pupils will become aware of the efficacy of the methods. Gone are the days when pupils lived in fear of their teacher, but there will be times when you have to pick up the pieces of a failing relationship between a pupil and his/her teacher. As time goes on, behaviour management may become an issue for the team and there will need to be a full discussion on the team approach.

You will occupy a pivotal role in the life of the team and the development of the subject or pastoral team. You will also be a member of the school staff. The role of the middle manager is discussed fully in Chapter 5. It is important to recognise that whilst you are the leader of the team, it is not the only team in the school and there are others who have a similar role. Further, in secondary schools, the middle manager leading a subject will normally be a form tutor and as such be part of a pastoral team – the pastoral leader will be part of a subject team. In a primary school, a coordinator will also be a class teacher and so on. This point is made to illustrate the interdependency of the teaching staff and as such the new middle manager needs to spend time getting to know all of their colleagues. In addition, there are the ancillary staff with whom the manager will interact; they are important to the life of the school and positive relationships need to be cultivated.

There is no hiding the fact that the first few weeks and months of middle management are characterised by hard work and persistent interaction with pupils and staff. However, over time the relationships which the teacher cherished at the previous school are replaced by good relationships built up at the new school. This is the induction process for the middle manager.

Dealing with a team member who also applied for your job

In some cases you will have to work with a member of the team who also applied for the job. This can be very difficult and there are several factors to consider here.

1 In the main, any resentment will not be direct towards you, because it is not your fault! Most teachers recognise this. Any resentment or hostility will come from hurt pride or a failure on the senior management part to adequately debrief the teacher.

2 It is worthwhile, therefore, asking the headteacher how this teacher responded to the debrief and to seek his/her advice.

3 The teacher may be watchful and wary. Some may watch to see if you fail. The sensitive middle manager acknowledges the hurt and treats the teacher with courtesy, but is also guarded. Your processes and interactions will need to be proper. This is not only for their own sake, but also to obviate any sense of '*I could have done better*'.

4 If the teacher is serious about promotion, you can help the teacher, in a sensitive manner, to prepare for such a role. This needs to be undertaken with care.

In general, teachers are accommodating people who recognise one another's strengths. If you are to be successful, you will have to prove yourself to all – this includes the headteacher, senior management, team members (supportive or otherwise), other staff, pupils, parents and so on. By demonstrating an awareness of feelings and a sensitive approach, you will already have learnt a valuable lesson in people management.

Setting the agenda for the first few months

The objectives of the first few weeks are to give yourself the opportunity to get to know the team and to establish yourself both as the leader and as a teacher. However, as time goes on you will wish, and be expected, to set an agenda for the changes you will bring about. The reason why it is important to wait before embarking on a major change is that until you know the strengths of the team, the development you lead will be yours alone. By getting to know the strengths of the team, you can use their interests as a means of engaging support.

There is one situation, however, where it is impossible to wait. This is in the case of a failing school or failing subject area. Under these circumstances, you are dealing directly with the headteacher and will not be given the comparative luxury of getting to know the team before you act. In this case you need to be very clear on your purpose and be sure of your methods. In many ways the methods are the same; they rely on a leader with a clearly articulated philosophy who acts in a principled manner. However, where the team is hostile to you the sharing of your philosophy at that opening meeting may have to be tempered or even saved for another occasion.

You may have no choice about the actions you have to take. However, in the long term, decisive and assertive strategies will have only a limited impact if a principled leader and effective manager does not deliver them. Delivering a difficult message is not an excuse for roughshod treatment of people. It is our view that being assertive and proactive is synonymous with principled leadership. Being horrid and unpleasant is not. There are times when managers have to say unpleasant things – you may have to tell a teacher that his/her teaching is unsatisfactory and that you recommend competency procedures – but this does not have to be done in an aggressive or unpleasant manner. This is the mark of a professional manager.

Taking care of yourself

In these first few months you will be under a good deal of stress. For most people, changing a job is one of the most stressful experiences. It follows closely behind death, divorce and moving house. It is important for the new middle manager to try to avoid additional stresses. Whilst one cannot always predict the events which shape our lives, there are steps we can take to minimise our stress levels.

A crucial factor for most people is the quality of their personal relationships. Whilst it may be tempting to embark on a new phase in one's career when a relationship comes to an end, it will be difficult to sustain oneself and the necessary emotional energy required for the new job, if outside of school, one's personal life is in tatters. Further, when establishing oneself in a new job, it is difficult to know who can be spoken to in confidence; and it is bad for a team's morale if their new manager is emotionally exhausted. It is surely better counsel to delay a new job until the emotional demands are lessened and all one's energy is devoted to the job.

Similarly, there are events which do fall beyond our control such as illness and bereavement. But teachers need to consider their lives carefully before embarking on the promotional ladder – the opportunities will be there in the future, and you do yourself no favours by trying to combine the care of a relative, the birth of a baby or indeed moving house, with a demanding new job.

When in post, you need to take your own health seriously and achieve a balance in your life. It is important to keep healthy and if playing squash or going to the gym or walking the dog is part of that healthy lifestyle, you need to maintain these activities. Also, it is easy to take health for granted and to neglect oneself in terms of diet, fitness and relaxation. The balance comes from being fit to do the job. Anyone involved in education will appreciate the enormity of the task and that the drive for perfection is never ending. However, by prioritising the needs of the pupil, the team and oneself, a balance can be struck. If you really think that you cannot take an hour to go and play squash, you need to look at how the work is being organised.

There are strategies for balancing the demands of home and school. Some of these include:

- engaging a partner's support and agreeing the division of domestic chores
- paying for a cleaner or other domestic help
- bartering time with friends to organise childcare
- organising reliable childcare
- using the Internet to do the shopping, etc.
- planning time to do things such as playing squash, socialising, etc. and sticking to it.

All successful middle managers have to make appropriate judgements and compromise their personal and professional lives; it is a question of balance. We can get the things done that we value and we should value ourselves most highly of all.

Leading change

One of the most important aspects of the middle manager's job is to lead effective change.

Change is fundamental to the education process and over recent years could be described as endemic. A classic definition of the change process is a linear model:

$$\text{objectives} \rightarrow \text{content} \rightarrow \text{organisation} \rightarrow \text{evaluation.}$$

Put simply, we decide what we want to achieve (i.e. what the objectives are), then decide on how we are going to do it (i.e. what the outcomes will be), then consider the organisation of the objectives (i.e. how we shall do it) and then finally evaluate the exercise. This model has been adapted to become more of a cyclical one; i.e. the evaluation is part of the change process in itself and the act of evaluation informs the change process. The change process is also a continuous one and this, in some ways, is the cause of its difficulties in school.

Many schools will be engaged in managing multiple changes, and this raises major curriculum planning issues which will need to be considered fully later.

Objectives-based models are, despite their wide use, open to a number of objections because they are considered as mechanistic. There is a feeling that schools do not function in this way. Schools are cultural organisations and change is a difficult thing to bring about. If we are to accept the notion that a school is a cultural organisation, there are several characteristics we need to consider in relation to the change process.

TASK 16

Identifying cultural characteristics

Using Table 3.7 below, identify the characteristics of your school and what makes them evident.

Think about how these characteristics have come about. What makes them endure?

What type of cultural resistance do you witness at school and how does the school respond to this resistance?

Include other characteristics that apply to your school.

TABLE 3.7 Cultural characteristics

Characteristic	Identifier	Resistance	Response of the school
School uniform	■ All children wear school sweatshirt and tie ■ Girls wear skirts ■ Boys wear trousers ■ ■	■ Children wear their tie improperly ■ Children wear a different sweatshirt ■ Girls campaign for trousers	■ Staff spend time telling children to tie their ties properly, tuck shirts in, remove sweatshirts
School assembly or other large gathering			
Staff meetings			
Relationships between staff and parents			
Relationships between staff and students			
Relationships between staff			
Rules and sanctions			
Reward systems			

The culture of a school is the way things are done. It goes beyond the outward signs and includes such matters as the attitude to classrooms – are they seen as an individual teacher's space? In some schools the classroom is a named teacher's domain and permission to enter is asked for. The lesson can be fiercely guarded as an interaction between the teacher and the class and to observe the lesson requires, again, the seeking of permission. In reality, however, the line manager and the teacher play a game where the teacher cannot refuse and the line manager does not have to ask – this is the nature of interaction in some schools.

However, one of the main objections to the linear process of change is that a school is an interactive place. It relies on the complex interactions between groups of adults and pupils. The nature of human interaction is such that it is not rigid; it is complex and complicated. Change management needs to acknowledge this and change becomes a process.

Another way of thinking of this linear model is to consider:

1 What educational purposes should we seek to achieve?

2 What educational experiences can we provide that are likely to achieve these purposes?

3 How can these educational experiences be effectively organised?

4 How can we determine whether these purposes are being achieved?

The major issue at this level, for the middle manager is where do these objectives come from? In some cases the objectives derive from benchmark data which suggests that standards need to be raised – but this does not really answer the question. Also, the issue with the evaluative part of the model is that some observable change in behaviour would need to happen before the achievement of the objective. Consequently all objectives would need to be expressed in behaviour terms rather than educational ones. The point here is that strategic change cannot always be measured in a meaningful way; there are indicators which point to improvement but these, in themselves, may not be accurate measures of the intended outcomes.

For middle managers, the strategic change they will lead will fall into several categories and these are illustrated in Table 3.8.

TABLE 3.8 Categories of middle manager-led strategic change

Category	Example	Measures
Skill-based	■ Staff are able to deliver a new aspect of the curriculum, e.g. use ICT as part of the scheme of work in Geography. ■ The school is delivering the Numeracy hour.	This could be measured in terms of the actual delivery of ICT, by producing a timetable for the delivery, etc. But is only by a qualitative assessment of the teaching, and sampling of the work produced, that the skill-based strategic change can be assessed.

Category	Example	Measures
Performance-based	■ There is an improvement in the pass rate at 'A' Level in an FE college. ■ There is an improvement in the reading ages of 5-year-old children.	The percentages for each of the subject areas could be compared with previous year's but there is a need to use baseline figures to make any assessment valid. The improvement in pass rates does not necessarily mean that the measures put in place have led to the increase. The manager needs to consider the outcomes with greater care.
Knowledge-based	■ Pupils know how to use the Internet. ■ History pupils know about the consequences of the Napoleonic wars.	These are knowledge-based objectives and can be measured using a test. However, the question arises: how long does a pupil need to retain the knowledge to meet this objective? If the pupil knows the facts at the end of the lesson, is this success? If they are unable to recall the facts the next lesson, is this failure?
Attitude-based	■ Pupils have a positive attitude to attending school.	Attendance figures and truancy rates can be useful, but an attitudinal survey would be needed.
Cultural	■ Pupils are dropping less litter in school. ■ Pupils are wearing a new school uniform. ■ Pupils are choosing to study ICT at GCSE.	Cultural change is difficult to quantify. A manager will not wish to count pieces of litter! The change that is required is the 'feeling that litter should not be

Category	Example	Measures
	■ Pupils are choosing GNVQ at FE college.	dropped' or 'pupils feel proud of their uniform and want to wear it'. This example illustrates the complexity of strategic change.

Strategic change is not just about setting objectives and organising events and measuring the results – it is a more subtle process. In order that strategic change brings about a lasting change, it has to embrace the existing culture of the school and move forward in a planned way. It is not haphazard. However, it recognises that it is people that bring about strategic change. There are several issues we need to consider in this context.

Determining the need for change

How do we determine the need for change? This is quite a hard question to answer, because in some cases it is obvious – improvements in the reading ages of 7 year olds at the school need to be made. However, whilst a programme which seeks to bring about these improvements can be set up and the outcomes clearly specified, it will not be lasting change unless the features which underpin the change become part of the practice of those who teach reading.

Determining the need for change can be difficult, particularly if you, as the manager are the only one who recognises this need. It is important, therefore, that as part of the process of leading change that you engage the support of the senior management team in the school or college. It is vital for the success of the change that you are supported. It can be lonely and difficult to lead a change when there is no one following; you need the support and encouragement of your superiors.

Change models

Change has to become part of the custom and practice of the school; in this way the staff and pupils take ownership of the matter. You need to recognise that your role is to lead and manage the change – it is not to do all the work. Your role is visionary in that you see what needs to be done and are able to bring about 'followership' on the part of the team. Your role is also functional, in that you devise a process where the actions are completed and the objectives met.

This can be quite hard to do. However, there are change models which are useful to consider and will form a good basis for strategic planning. The model for strategic change shown in Table 3.9 is based on Gibbons (1977). There are seven major stages in the model; each stage has its own kind of task, its own kind of process and its own product.

TABLE 3.9 Model for strategic change

Task	Process	Product
1. *Identify* what job the curriculum has to do.	*Analyse* the situation.	A clear *purpose* for curriculum development.
2. *Formulate* a means of achieving the purpose.	*Design* a curriculum concept.	A promising *theoretical model* of the curriculum.
3. Select an appropriate *teaching strategy* for the curriculum.	*Establish* principles of procedure for students and teachers when using the curriculum.	A specific teaching/*learning* strategy.
4. *Produce* the curriculum delivery system.	*Develop* the means required to present and maintain the curriculum.	An *operational* curriculum.
5. *Experiment* with the curriculum on student learning and the school.	*Refine* the model through classroom research and regular improvements.	A *refined* curriculum.
6. *Implement* the curriculum throughout the school in other settings.	*Change* general practice to the new curriculum.	A *widely used* curriculum.
7. *Evaluate* the effects of the curriculum on student learning.	*Evaluate* how effective the curriculum is.	A *proven* curriculum.

The emphasis here is on a dynamic process which is not intransigent. It is responsive; it is evaluative and is driven by change itself. However, your task is to translate this model into a process that you can use to plan your work.

CASE STUDY 1

Planning change

Louise is Head of Year in a comprehensive school. She is concerned that the children find it difficult to study effectively. As part of the pastoral team, Louise has been given the objective of improving study skills for children in the school. She recognises that a change to current practice will be needed to achieve this objective.

This case study will be used to illustrate how a middle manager can plan strategic change in order to meet an objective.

TABLE 3.10 Planning change

Task	Process	Product
1. *Identify.* Here Louise needs to identify what needs to be done and she will be able to do this by finding out about the existing practices and the problems these create. She identifies that an improvement in the ability of children to study is required.	*Analyse.* By conducting some kind of audit of study skills Louise will be able to find out about existing good practice and the outcomes it produces. By examining the demands of the curriculum as a whole she can see where the gaps in this aspect of the curriculum are.	*Purpose.* The purpose for the development is clear: to improve study skills. However, by clear identification of the needs of the children and the issues raised by the deficiencies in the curriculum, the purpose of the development is clarified.
2. *Formulate.* At this stage Louise can work with others to consider a range of possible ways of delivering a study skills programme. She may decide that it should be delivered as part of the tutorial programme or in a cross-curricular mode. However, the formulation of the programme will be	*Design.* By designing an appropriate model for the delivery of study skills based on existing good practice and the needs of the children, Louise embraces the present with the future. This is good practice because it starts from where the school is and looks forward to where	*Theoretical model.* By spending time finding out and planning on the basis of pupil need and curriculum strength, the emphasis for the programme will evolve naturally. By focusing on the strengths and weaknesses, others will be able to work with Louise to develop appropriate

Task	Process	Product
facilitated by the information she found in the identification stage.	it wants to be.	teaching strategies.
3. *Teaching strategy.* Louise works with her team to consider how they are going to deliver study skills as part of the tutorial programme. She invites middle managers with curriculum responsibility to join the group to consider how the teaching programme in core subjects can support the study skills programme she is designing.	*Establish.* At this stage the strategic principles for this new curriculum are clear: it is a cross-curricular programme and a tutorial programme delivered to support one another. By establishing this at the outset, the planning becomes more productive.	A specific teaching/*learning* strategy.
4. *Produce.* Now Louise is able to work with the group to devise teaching programmes. The group uses the needs analysis undertaken at the start and plans around these. Subject representatives will be able to commit their teams to supporting the delivery in the tutorial programme because it will support their work. The children will be supported in their learning because of the coherence this model depends upon.	*Develop.* The materials are prepared and the programme for delivery is set out. Because there has been a strong focus on the needs of the children, the outcomes will be generated by the programme itself. Louise and other leaders will need to train staff to use the materials effectively and the programme will need to be explained to the children so that they can engage fully in the programme.	*Operational.* At this stage the curriculum is being delivered. The staff are trained, the materials produced, the children are involved.

Task	Process	Product
5. *Experiment*. This is a new programme and so the outcomes may not match the intention, i.e. things go wrong! Louise will plan into the meetings an opportunity for the team to share their experiences. Where things are good, there is occasion for celebration. The parts which go wrong are analysed and put right.	*Refine* the model through classroom research and regular improvements.	*Refined*. The mode of operation is tailored to the desired outcomes and the needs of the team.
6. *Implement*. Having planned and delivered a programme, successes and experiences can be shared with others. The team has included core subject managers; the next stage is to develop a whole curriculum approach to study skills and to promulgate the results throughout the school.	*Change*. The curriculum has developed to embrace the needs of the children. It started by identifying good practices and needs.	A *widely used* curriculum. The programme can 'embed' itself into schemes of work and become part of the curriculum. It has been developed by a group and so will enjoy wide ownership.
7. *Evaluate the effects* of the curriculum on student learning. Louise needs to undertake some form of review with the group. She can involve the children in this review, as they were made aware of the process being developed for and with them.	*Evaluate* how effective the curriculum is.	A *proven* curriculum. The curriculum started from the needs of the children and has developed their skills. The proof lies in the obvious improvements. In the long term there will be improvements in the levels of attainment the children reach.

This process can be adapted to suit any middle manager's agenda. However, there are several points to consider when planning a strategic change.

1. *Timing* – one of the characteristics of schools over the past ten years or so has been the plethora of new initiatives. It is not uncommon for teachers to denounce proposed change simply because it is change. In some organisations there is change fatigue. However, we consider that an important part of the process is ensuring that the change is realistic and needed. If teachers recognise the need for the change and the plan is a realistic one, most will be supportive.

2. *Plan small steps and concentrate on the details* – the initiative for many of the changes going on in schools belongs to the Government and Local Education Authority. Whole school development issues drive other initiatives. Whilst these may put middle managers into a reactive state, their responsibility is still to lead the change in a calm and proactive manner. By spending time planning the small steps and concentrating on the details, middle managers will demonstrate a high level of both interpersonal and organisational skill. The ability to judge exactly how long it will take to produce a set of resources will be valuable and will increase the initiative's chance of success. However, a rushed, poorly-managed project with no time for completion, or a piece of work which loses momentum will not achieve its objectives.

3. *Celebrate success and share good practice* – when the steps are completed successfully, it is important that the middle manager celebrates this with the team. A brief hand-written note will do wonders to keep the project on track. Telling the rest of the team when a stage is completed will maintain motivation. However, if things start to go awry and a stage is in danger of missing its deadline, then you will need to consider your reaction carefully. In some cases insistence on the deadline will bring out the best in those who respond well to pressure. However, this is not the time for threats! You will need to be tenacious but in a controlled way. If the cost of achieving the long-term objective is a stage deadline then the project is worth pursuing.

4. *Evaluate as you go along* – teachers will continue to work on a project if it is of benefit to the pupils they teach. However, if the objectives have to change or the materials are not working, it is important that the project manager responds accordingly. The judgement comes from deciding when to be tenacious and rigid and when to be malleable and persuaded. These are professional judgements.

Effective project management is one of the most fulfilling aspects of middle management. It is a time when you will work closely with a small group of people (compared with the project management of a senior manager working with a much larger group). As such it is an opportunity to develop these skills. It is a time to learn about creating and managing systems. It is a time to learn about effective delegation and trust. There will be times when the project goes awry: such an occurrence needs to be regarded with a degree of pragmatism and a great deal of realism. For the most part, in schools things can be put right – they may cause inconvenience and expense and disharmony – but they can be rectified and the experience can be a profitable one.

Time management

Classroom teachers have a good level of control over their working day. The unpredictable nature of working with people – especially children – is a factor when measuring the amount of control, but for the most part, their job is to teach their classes.

However, middle managers have to both teach their own classes and manage the team and this purpose of this section is to discuss ways of coping with the wide variety of events that appear during a typical day. The important point to stress at this stage is that a middle manager's role is to *manage* problems – not always to *solve* problems for others. If you try to do this you will be a poorer manager as a result simply because you will have too much to do and spend your time being reactive rather than proactive.

TASK 17

Urgent v. important

What is important? What is urgent? Write a definition of each of these.

Read Table 3.11 which is a list of events in this head of English Department's day. Categorise the events as urgent, non-urgent, important and non-important.

Are there any events that she could have anticipated?

How should she respond to each event?

TABLE 3.11 Events in the day of the head of English

Event	Urgent/Important	Response
1. Arrives at school to find out that a teacher is ill and has set work for her classes.		
2. There are seven envelopes in the post for her to open.		
3. Memo from the Head asking for information on last year's GCSE syllabus.		
4. The representative from a publishing house is calling to discuss requirements for the next academic year at lunchtime.		
5. Details of the plays being staged at the local theatre have arrived.		
6. It is her turn for break duty.		
7. During lesson 2 (just before break) a boy is sent to her class saying he has been sent out from Mr Jones's class. He has no work to do and doesn't know why he has been sent out.		
8. There is a curriculum review meeting straight after school.		
9. There is a note from the Deputy Head saying that a complaint about an English teacher has been received and he needs to discuss it today.		
10. One of the English staff is working on a unit of work for Year 10 Poetry and wants some feedback on what they have produced so far.		

This would be quite a busy day but it illustrates the need to have effective strategies for managing situations as they arrive. There are a number of ways in which the Head of Department could respond and these are discussed in Table 3.12.

TABLE 3.12 The head of English's response

Event	Response
1. Arrives at school to find out that a teacher is ill and has set work for her classes.	If the system for absent staff is well known, simply checking that classes are all right at the start of each lesson is sufficient. A policy where staff phone you with work might be needed. Also, it is important to have a set of 'Emergency Work' for such an instance.
2. There are seven envelopes in the post for her to open.	Quickly scan the envelopes – any addressed to the Head of English are usually circulars and can be left for another time. Hand-written envelopes are often from parents and should receive a response during the day. If there is no money for purchasing, then there is little point in reading catalogues or circulars.
3. Memo from the Head asking for information on last year's GCSE syllabus.	Depending on the amount of detail required, the manager can respond instantly (by return of memo) or write a holding response.
4. The representative from a publishing house is calling to discuss requirements for the next academic year at lunchtime.	Agree a time with the representative. Ensure that the representative knows what you want to discuss. It is a good idea to arrange the meeting so that it is forced to end by the bell for afternoon school.
5. Details of the plays being staged at the local theatre have arrived.	Take this home to read or pass to another person in the department whose role it is to organise such trips.
6. During lesson 2 (just before break) a boy is sent to the class saying he has been sent out from Mr Jones's class. He has no work to do and	Give the boy a piece of paper and tell him to write down what has happened. Carry on teaching. At a convenient point read his statement and either a) arrange for him to apologise or b) say that you will have to meet with the teacher also to sort the problem out and that his parents will need to be informed. It is amazing how many

Event	Response
doesn't know why he has been sent out.	problems resolve themselves! However, you will need to see Mr Jones about this incident. Department policy may need to be amended so that if children are sent out of class they have work to do.
7. It is her turn for break duty.	You have to do this and should not shirk from this important task.
8. There is a curriculum review meeting straight after school.	Plan for this meeting by reading the notes and any necessary preparation the night before.
9. There is a note from the Deputy Head saying that a complaint about an English teacher has been received and he needs to discuss this today.	Write to the Deputy and say that you are free after the curriculum review meeting or suggest another time.
10. One of the English staff is working on a unit of work for Year 10 Poetry and wants some feedback on what they have produced so far.	When organising the work with the team arrange the deadline in advance. Ask the teacher to give you a sample of the work, with notes to explain what he has done and you will review it for the next day.

The ability to manage yourself and the team is a skill which takes time to acquire and needs to be practised. However, by trying to be calm and measured in your response, the outcomes are likely to be better.

There are a number of adages which can be useful to consider when organising a day:

1 *More haste less speed* – it is important to work hard, but trying to do too many things usually result in either things going wrong or jobs not done to satisfaction.

2 *A stitch in time saves nine* – tackling small problems as they arise requires less time and effort than letting them escalate into big problems.

3 *Try to handle each piece of paper once* – this is hard to do! However, if you can train yourself to respond rather than to carry memos and the like about with you, it is quite an achievement!

4 *If it isn't broken, don't try to fix it* – sometimes by doing nothing a problem will resolve itself. Occasionally, intervening can make a problem worse – this is the value of experience and advice.

5 *It is better to lose the battle and win the war* – in the grand scheme of things, it may be better to give way over minor issues and save the intransigence for the important ones.

Managing a team is challenging and those who execute their duties successfully have to learn hard lessons. The first lessons will come in the first few weeks when the transition is made from classroom teacher to middle manager. It is important to reflect on these experiences. They are there to learn from. Among the staff there will be others who have had similar experiences; it is important to find peers in whom you can trust. The need for support can be great and having those who understand the pressures will be a huge comfort. Remember too the headteacher and senior managers in the school – they are there to support your work and they want to know what you are doing. The senior management team will have been middle managers at some time during their careers and the voice of experience can be a source of valuable counsel and encouragement.

———— Summary ————

Our intention is that at the end of this chapter you will:

- have analysed the new post
- have considered the etiquette for leaving your current post
- have prepared for the first meeting with the Headteacher
- have prepared for the first meeting with the team
- be prepared to interview and observe all the members of the team
- be able to create a team profile
- be able to manage the stress of the new role and manage your time efficiently
- understand the change process and be able to implement strategic change.

chapter four

Developing a vision

What are leadership and management?

Power and authority

Management models

Developing a vision

Communicating the vision

Constructing a development plan

Making sure the development plan is carried out

Summary

One of the more challenging aspects to the middle manager's role is to lead the team. The word 'leadership' has come into management parlance over recent years and it is presumed that those in a management role know what it implies. This chapter is about defining leadership and management. Further it is about how to develop a vision for the task that is middle management.

This chapter is divided into sections which deal with:

- what leadership and management are
- how to develop a vision for your team's work
- how to communicate that vision
- how to construct a development plan
- how to link your improvement planning to whole school development
- monitoring the development plan – making sure it gets done.

———— What are leadership ———— and management?

There have been several attempts to define leadership and to try to separate it from management. One of the more prominent American writers Wess Roberts (1989) stated a number of 'secrets' for leaders in *The Leadership Secrets of Attila the Hun*. These statements form the basis of the next task.

TASK 18
Are you a good leader?

Read through the 'Secrets' listed in Table 4.1 and consider to what extent they apply to the middle manager.

What are the implications for you as a person and as a middle manager?

TABLE 4.1 Secrets of leadership

'Secret'	What the secret means for the role of the middle manager	Personal effect	Professional effect
Kings should always appoint their best huns as chieftains, no matter how much they are needed in their current position.	■ This statement is about recognising the worth of those in your team. Sometimes the middle manager has to make judgements to deploy their staff and this may mean moving someone who is doing an excellent job to another role. ■ Further, a middle manager has the responsibility to develop skills in their team; the effect of this will be to prepare people for promotion (and leaving the team).		
Never appoint acting chieftains. Put the most capable hun in charge, give him both responsibility and authority, and then hold him accountable.	■ When the middle manager is appointed, the middle manager is the most capable hun. ■ This secret is one of the paradoxes of middle management. The responsibility for the subject or the particular team is yours and the accountability is also yours. However, because of the nature of power and authority in schools, this aspect of the role will always be problematic.		

'Secret'	What the secret means for the role of the middle manager	Personal effect	Professional effect
	This is explored in the text following this table.		
A wise chieftain never depends on luck. Rather he always trusts his future to hard work, stamina, tenacity and a positive attitude.	■ This is an important point and is the subject of this book in general and this chapter in particular. ■ An essential attribute of a successful middle manager is the ability to recognise that it is hard work sustained over a period of time that makes for effective work. However, as this chapter will demonstrate, effective leadership is not just about hard work – it is the ability to work with people and for people and for this to be reciprocated.		

'Secret'	What the secret means for the role of the middle manager	Personal effect	Professional effect
A wise chieftain knows he is responsible for the welfare of his huns and acts accordingly.	■ In the centre of all that we do in schools are teachers and students. ■ Middle managers have to remind themselves that they are working with people and for people. No manager is successful if the consequences of his/her endeavour cannot be expressed in the changes they made to people's lives.		
Being a leader of the huns is often a lonely job.	■ This is true. ■ In challenging roles, the loneliness can be extreme, but the vision and the desire to create life chances for students are the motives to carry on.		
Shared risk-taking will weld the relationship of a chieftain and his huns.	■ Although the middle manager has the responsibility and		

'Secret'	What the secret means for the role of the middle manager	Personal effect	Professional effect
	the accountability for the team, the middle manager also creates and sustains the team through his/her leadership. ■ The ability to lead a group of people to a stage where they do things differently is the mark of success.		
A chieftain can never be in charge if he rides in the rear.	■ This is a truism. A strong leader will show the way forward. The middle manager will not always lead every time because the middle manager will recognise the expertise of others and the need for others to experience leadership, but the middle manager will be there and his/her influence will be tangible.		

These 'secrets' are at the heart of effective leadership. Leadership is about knowing the way forward and being able to see the future. It is a creative and liberating process. Management is about ensuring that the systems are in place and that the team fulfils the obligations of the process. Management is a function of leadership. Without leadership, management is sterile and has limited success; without management, leadership is 'hot-air' and failed dreams.

The 'secrets' illustrate how middle managers have to consider their work. Middle managers have to look to the future and have a strong belief in what needs to be done; however, they must also have the sense to develop effective strategies for realising the vision. This is the professional middle manager.

Power and authority

The nature of power and authority is an important concept that needs to be discussed. Bush (1989) articulated a number of models for school management. These were as listed in Table 4.2.

TABLE 4.2 Bush's models of power and authority in schools

1 *Bureaucratic* – this is where there is a clear-cut division of labour. What characterises a bureaucratic school are rules, regulations and a strong sense of hierarchy.

2 *Collegial* – the decisions are based on the professional discretion of the teachers. The characteristics of a collegial school are committees and a culture when policies emerge resulting from discussion and debate.

3 *Political* – in this organisation power is centralised and the culture is one in a state of conflict.

4 *Subjective* – this model derives from what people do. In this organisation, each individual has a subjective perception of the organisation and process and behaviour are key characteristics.

5 *Ambiguous* – this model stresses the uncertainty and complexity of an institution's life.

It would be too simplistic to ask you to try to match each of these models with your own school. As theory has developed, one of the most enlightening conclusions has been that organisations do not fit into management theory boxes. Rather, the organisation is complex and complicated. Aspects of the organisation may be bureaucratic, but they depend on collegiality for their maintenance. We develop this idea further in the following case study.

CASE STUDY

Summertown Primary School

Summertown Primary School is a good school. It has 12 teachers and a roll of 380. It was recently inspected and the report described it as well-managed. However, the school has made only a small improvement in its Key Stage 1 and Key Stage 2 results. The results compare reasonably with other schools but given that the quality of the teaching was found to be at least good in 95 per cent of the lessons, the question arises as to why results are not better. The head of infant school, the literacy coordinator and the numeracy leader have been asked to develop an action plan in response to the report.

This case study highlights a number of issues in this consideration of management theory. The school is described as 'well-managed'. It has good systems for dealing with the day-to-day issues of running a school. In that sense, it is a bureaucratic organisation. Indeed the titles of the three people working on the action plan illustrate the hierarchical nature of the school's management system. The question which arises from this case study and indeed, the problem which confronts these three postholders is: why isn't the school doing better? The scenario is one which faces all schools when they receive a similar report.

The answer is complex.

The solution is not only about management but also about leadership. The management of schools is essentially problematic. The models outlined earlier in this chapter are simplistic in the sense that they cannot possibly attempt to describe or explain the nature of management in schools. This is because a school is not a homogenous entity which can be controlled by rigid systems. Why? Because a school is a living organisation – it is full of children and students at various stages in their development. The development of children into adults is not linear and the next task is to consider the constraints that this places on a school.

TASK 19

Constraints on progress

Consider the ways in which children develop in the phase of education in which you work.

What constraints does this place on the way in which the children can progress?

What effect does this have on the planning that teachers undertake?

Include any other aspects of development you consider important.

To complete this analysis Table 4.3 categorises the aspects of development. We have stated one aspect to help you to complete the others:

TABLE 4.3 Aspects of children's development and their implications

Development	Characteristics and markers (or stages)	Constraints for interaction	Planning Issues
Cognitive	■ sequencing ■ sorting ■ classifying ■ comparing ■ predicting ■ cause and effect ■ concluding ■ creating ■ problem solving ■ deciding ■ analysing ■ synthesising	■ Key Stage tests ■ public examinations ■ physical environment ■ cultural constraints ■ resourcing	■ mixed ability teaching ■ setting ■ streaming ■ activity-based learning ■ organisation of physical environment ■ planning for use of resources ■ strategic curriculum development ■ planning for assessment ■ using assessment to plan the curriculum ■ integrating the curriculum
Spatial	■	■	■
Oral	■	■	■

Development	Characteristics and markers (or stages)	Constraints for interaction	Planning Issues
Conceptual	■	■	■
Social	■	■	■
Physical	■	■	■
Spiritual	■	■	■
Moral	■	■	■

By considering the stages or aspects of children's development in this way, we appreciate not only the complexity of the task, but also the opportunities it offers. For example, as middle managers organising an aspect of the curriculum it is important that the curriculum is planned and that it is consistent with children's development. Further, the curriculum needs to be cohesive, in that it cannot be disparate nor subject to fits and starts – it has to have continuity and make sense. The opportunity presented to the middle managers in this case study is precisely the chance to create a curriculum which is coherent and cohesive. Management systems underpin a led curriculum but they are no substitute for strong leadership.

This is a difficult aspect of middle management. (Indeed the term management itself is part of the problem!) But it is not unattainable. However, any middle manager needs to appreciate not only the need to develop strong systems for managing a team, but also the importance of a vision for the role and a sense of direction.

Management models

Before we discuss the idea of direction further, we shall consider how the models of management can be applied to the middle manager's role. There is a space to include your own notes.

TABLE 4.4 Management models and the middle manager

Model and characteristic	Applied to the middle manager's role	Examples	Your notes
1. Bureaucratic	■ It is necessary to have policies on aspects of the team's work. ■ Financial responsibility rests with the team leader. ■ Line management responsibility rests with the team leader.	■ Marking and assessment policy ■ Job descriptions ■ Supervision rotas ■ Arrangements for appraisal and performance review	

Model and characteristic	Applied to the middle manager's role	Examples	Your notes
2. Collegial	■ Organisation of meetings ■ How resources are used ■ There is a team opinion.	■ Meetings have an agenda, but there is opportunity for quality discussion which leads to team decisions. ■ Staff are encouraged to work together to produce resources. ■ All of the team are involved in the practice of policy.	
3. Political	■ There is a desire to move forward and to challenge accepted norms. ■ Middle managers have to ask themselves whether such a model is desirable to embody in their teams.	■ Staff who are entrenched in a particular view or mode of operation may respond, for a time, to a conflict. This can have the effect of clearing the air.	
4. Subjective	■ The manager can identify the dominant characteristics of individual teachers' work and build up a profile of opinion and expertise. ■ This model is about what people do and how they behave.	■ Individual interviews held regularly to discuss the work the teacher is doing. ■ Personalised job descriptions ■ Identifying staff who will have a particular view and utilising the potential.	

Model and characteristic	Applied to the middle manager's role	Examples	Your notes
	■ It emphasises the need to change behaviour in those whom the manager seeks to lead.		
5. Ambiguous	■ Recognising that there are many ways to describe a team's work and that the manager needs to be responsive to changing circumstances.	■ Use of working documents ■ Updating schemes of work and resources regularly ■ Planning on the basis of change	

———— Developing a vision ————

In many ways the ability to give a team direction is the most challenging aspect of the middle manager's role. Some people are by nature visionary – they can see the future; or at least can convince others that their view will be the all-pervading one. Others are only able to deal with the here-and-now but their strength lies in the systems they manage. Without effective management a vision will remain unfulfilled; without leadership, a team's work can become at best dull, at worst reactive.

In some ways for learning to become visionary is impossible but Task 20 is designed to help you think through the issues which affect the team's remit.

TASK 20 ————————————————————————

Identifying influences on your team's work

In Table 4.5 below are some questions which require you to consider the influences on your team's work over the past three years.

Consider the local influences, those in your school.

Consider the national picture – what indicators do you have for the future of your team's work? Give reasons for your choices.

TABLE 4.5 Developing a sense of direction for your team's work

1. List the changes to your team's remit
over the past three years:

■ Curriculum

■ Knowledge

■ Methods of teaching

■ Modes of assessment

2. What National initiatives have affected
your team's work over the past three
years, e.g.:

■ Literacy

■ Numeracy

■ Key Stage curriculum changes

■ Qualification changes (e.g. A/S,
  GNVQ, etc.)

3. Look at curriculum statements which affect your team's remit – what changes are
planned for the next year or so?

4. Are these changes, in your view, the right ones? Do any professional bodies (such
as NAHT, NATE, ATMS, etc.) support or challenge the changes? What arguments
would you put forward to either support current initiatives or to propose alternatives?

5. What will be the implications for teaching and learning if the initiatives continue?

6. What training demands will these have on you, as middle manager? What training will your team require?

7. In three years' time how will your team need to operate to accommodate the changes? Will there be a need for team-teaching, moderation of coursework, liaison with other schools, ICT, etc.?

These questions can be used to create a long-term plan for your team. By thinking about recent developments and the effect that they have had on your team's work it is easier to see how it might develop. It is also very important to consider whether the changes have been for the better! A leader with vision will reflect on the impact that initiatives make and assess the qualitative effect. If, in their view, the direction is wrong or the initiative is flawed, they would feel a responsibility to the team and to the students to raise this with the senior management team and the school Governors. At this stage there needs to be a fully considered critique of the initiative and a suggested action plan. It is no good to dismiss ideas out of hand with nothing to replace them! This is educational vacuum. Of course, schools have to fulfil any legal requirements, but the support of a governing body when proposing any change of emphasis is crucial. Such action is professionally challenging, but is necessary to preserve the student's best interests.

———— Communicating the vision ————

The emphasis of the previous section has been for the middle manager to develop a vision for the subject or the particular remit of their role. However, it is imperative that the vision is communicated and shared with the team and the wider school community. Effective leadership of a team comes from a clear sense of purpose which has a vision at its root. The team need to know the vision and become part of it (although they may not all share the vision and may be against it – this will be discussed later).

There are several stages to an effective communication:

- analyse the needs of the team
- consider the strengths of the team and how they perceive their role
- analyse the implications of the vision for the team – will it require different ways of working?
- predict and manage the responses of the team
- prepare thoroughly to share with the team
- follow the meeting with documentation, plans and actions.

TASK 21

Communicating the vision to the team

For the new middle manager, this can seem quite a daunting task. However, the following algorithm is a way in which this process can be brought about; each of the above stages will be discussed in turn.

Use the questions in Table 4.6 to enable you to communicate your vision to your team.

---

1. Analyse the needs of the team

The purpose of this initial stage is to consider the needs of the team and to enable you to plan your work to accommodate the results of the analysis.

TABLE 4.6 The team's needs

Question	Response
1. Summarise the changes in the work of the team over the past two years.	In the two years the team has brought about the following changes: ■ ■ ■

Question	Response
2. How have the team responded to the changes? (Ofsted reports can be useful here.) Relate the responses to results at Key Stages, public examinations or other performance indicators.	The effect of these changes has been: ■ ■ ■ The evidence for this is: ■ ■ ■
3. What are the three main priorities for the team for the next year? Specify these in terms of actions and relate them to outcomes for students.	The priorities for the team over the next year are: 1. 2. 3. The outcomes for students will be: ■ ■ ■

By analysing the work of the team in this way, you can see clearly how the team has progressed. For a new middle manager, finding some of the information can be difficult. There are a number of sources of information which include:

■ Ofsted reports
■ annual reports to the headteacher

- reports to parents
- league tables
- development plans
- senior management team.

2. Consider the strengths of the team and how they perceive their role

Considering the strengths of the team is crucial to the success of any development work. In order for the team to develop, there needs to be an honest appraisal of the aspects of the job that the team does well and a candid assessment of what needs to be tackled. The planning which is necessary to bring about sustained improvement will be undermined without this consideration.

TABLE 4.7 Team strengths and weaknesses

List the members of your team	What teaching groups have they had over the past two years?	Measure the success of this teacher with these groups. Have they achieved target grades, what is the trend, etc.	What are the strengths of this teacher's work?	What targets does the teacher currently have?

It is useful to include yourself in this consideration. Whilst your are responsible for planning the development and ensuring that it happens, you are also an intrinsic part of the team and will demonstrate your leadership skills by ensuring that you have a fundamental role in bringing about development at all levels.

By assessing the team in this way, you have stated where the team is in terms of its potential; there may be reasons which explain any discrepancies or poor results and these have to be considered carefully. However, the focus for a visionary middle manager is the future and the improvements the middle manager will bring about through their own efforts and the efforts of others.

3. Analyse the implications of the vision for the team – will it require different ways of working?

Consider each element from Task 20 and Table 4.5 on pages 115 and 116.

TABLE 4.8 Implications of the vision

Element – list the curriculum changes which will affect your team's remit over the next few years.	What changes will these require? Consider:	What will need to happen? Compare this with existing practice.	How can this be brought about? List the elements of this assessment model.
	■ assessment ■ reporting ■ moderation ■ classroom practice ■ activities ■ teacher activity ■ ■		

At the end of this section you will have considered the various elements of the initiative and have considered what the implications are for the way the team will need to operate. It is important to do this stage without reference to the personalities involved and there are a number of reasons why this is the case:

- The team is not constant – teachers come and go and various times and situations change. Planning only with reference to the existing team can lead you into difficulties if the team changes.

- Thinking too deeply about the response of the team (which is the focus of the next section) at this stage can prevent you from considering all the possibilities; it is easy to say to yourself 'Miss Jones will never do that ...' and let that stand in the way of a good idea!

- At this level, the planning should be about ensuring the opportunities for students are maximised and the full requirements of any initiative are met.

4. Predict and manage the response of the team

Reactions to new initiatives can vary considerably and it is the mark of a good middle manager to anticipate these and plan their own responses accordingly.

What is important at this stage is to consider all the possible responses (in terms of objections, emotions, etc.) and then try to understand the basis for the response.

TASK 22

Managing responses

Table 4.9 lists some responses and the management issues. Include some of your own and consider the implications of such a response on your own planning.

TABLE 4.9　Predicting and managing team responses

Response	Possible basis for the response	How to manage this response	Possible implications for planning
Enthusiasm	■ Genuine belief that the initiative is required ■ Support for the team leader ■ Lip-service – the teacher	■ Plan for the enthusiast to be involved in the development ■ Plan the initiative so that all the team are involved	

Response	Possible basis for the response	How to manage this response	Possible implications for planning
	sounds supportive but plans to ignore the initiative or treat it cursorily	■ Ensure that full involvement is part of the planning and delivery	
Fatigue	■ Teachers may be fatigued with the changes that have occurred over recent years ■ Teachers may support it but add a rider that there is too much change, etc.	■ Difficult – what characterises education is constant change ■ Use the previous analysis to illustrate how change has led to improvement (if it has been the case) or point to other areas where a failure to change has been to the detriment of student opportunity	
Cynicism	■ Fear of change ■ Insecurity ■ Previous initiatives having been unsuccessful ■ Personal reasons	■ Effective planning and strong team management can alleviate fear ■ Ensuring that the change starts from 'where the team is' and is charted to 'where the team needs to be' in small planned steps can address fears	

Response	Possible basis for the response	How to manage this response	Possible implications for planning
		■ Personal reasons may need to be addressed by a private conversation	
Caution	■ Fear ■ Lack of confidence ■ Team dynamics	■ Teachers may respond cautiously because they do not see all the implications or may not wish to be regarded as unsupportive ■ You will need to look for signs of caution and respond	
Hostility	■ Frustration ■ Antipathy to you ■ Antipathy to the school ■ Fear ■ Disaffection	■ Some people love to argue! You need to anticipate possible objections and ensure that arguments against them are all in place. In this way you will be able to respond to the objections calmly and consistently. (It is sometimes worthwhile rehearsing these, if possible, with a trusted colleague)	

Response	Possible basis for the response	How to manage this response	Possible implications for planning
		■ There are some issues where it is pointless to argue! If there is no alternative or the direction has been given from the headteacher, the response can be swiftly delivered	

Dealing with hostility is not easy. It demands strength of character and a conviction that what is being done is the right thing to do. However, by anticipating the objections and the responses, a difficult meeting can be managed to good effect.

5. Prepare thoroughly to share with the team

There is no substitute for thorough preparation. Teams vary considerably and the objections raised and the manner in which they are manifested can be unrelated to the middle manager's role. They say more about the individual. However, to safeguard your position, you have to anticipate and plan.

Having completed all this work, you need to prepare for the meeting with the team. Normally, such meetings are part of directed time and as such are on a school calendar. If this is the case, then it is straightforward – the date and time are not an issue. However, if the school has not set out the meeting schedule, you should discuss the need for such meetings with the headteacher. Having agreed the need for a meeting, you should make the arrangements as follows.

■ Prepare an agenda which should include the following details:

- date, time and venue for the meeting
- apologies and Matters arising from the previous meeting
- the purpose of the meeting.

It is up to you to decide how much detail to include in the agenda, but good practice is to give teachers sufficient detail to enable them to think about the purpose of the meeting so that the discussion can be more fruitful. There is nothing worse than a meeting where no one has had a chance to think about far-reaching actions or where responses are off-the cuff or ill considered.

You may wish to alert people in the team to particular aspects of the meeting. Sometimes by thinking about the possible objections to the topics, any negative responses can be anticipated by having a discussion with an individual. Also, by raising issues with a person before the meeting, support can be created as the topic is debated.

6. Follow the meeting with documentation, plans and actions

After the meeting it is vital that the momentum you have worked to create is sustained. During the meeting, you will have introduced ideas and actions will need to have been agreed. Where these have been agreed and where the steps to bring about the development have been agreed, they should be recorded.

This is important for a number of reasons:

- In a busy school, it is easy to get caught up with the immediacy of everyday life and to neglect the need for development.
- The skill of a middle manager is about ensuring that the planned development happens.
- In the case of any dispute, the documentation is vital.

Within a short period of time, Minutes for the meeting should be published to the team; these Minutes should record the following:

- date, time and venue of the meeting
- who was present, absent
- apologies and Matters arising
- summary of the discussion on the topics on the agenda. Where there are action points, they should state what has to be done, by whom and by when.

It is not necessary to record every statement made. It is not a transcript! However, sufficient detail should be recorded to give a flavour of the discussion and the outcomes.

Constructing a development plan

Development plans in schools vary considerably in their format, but a good development plan should contain the following features:

- a review of the previous year's plan
- a statement of the priorities for the next year
- a response to whole school development targets
- a department or team improvement plan.

Table 4.10 is an example of a departmental improvement plan and can be used as a template.

TABLE 4.10 Improvement plan for a Mathematics department

Present situation for each year group	Intended development	Resources required	Costs £	Inset required to support developments	Cost £	Member of staff responsible for the development	Evidence of success related to Department Target
IMPROVEMENT 1 Standards of Numeracy vary considerably when pupils enter the school. Numeracy Hour begins in Primary school in September 1999	■ Programme of meetings on common themes with Primary School colleagues (Year 6 teachers and/or Mathematics coordinators). ■ To hold at least three meetings during the Academic Year. ■ Develop the 'Link' Project. Adler School Mathematics team to develop their links with 'their' school.	■ Photo-copying, postage, refresh-ments to service the meetings (twilight) ■ Use of Freed Time (negotiate with deputy team leader)	£100	■ Use Freed Time in June/July 2001 and January 2002 ■ Use of Strategies time	–	TEAM LEADER/all Department	■ Three meetings held over the Academic Year ■ Agreement across the phase on the Agenda – at least one item to be suggested and led by Primary staff ■ 80% of schools to be represented at each meeting ■ 90% of 'Link' Projects completed ■ At least two common projects (including the 'Link' Project undertaken by Adler and Primary School staff ■ All KS2 results to be sent to Adler School ■ All Adler staff to have visited their 'link' school at least once

TABLE 4.10 Continued

IMPROVEMENT 2				
The pace of lessons is recognised in school and nationally to be a factor in determining progress	■ To develop a series of opening/recap activities to start lessons. ■ To encourage staff to use opening activities and to see the benefits. ■ Develop the idea of a lesson format, which uses Stating activity, Development (on themed activities) and Plenary. ■ Lessons to be videotaped for discussion at Department meetings.	■ Photo-copying ■ Lesson Observation (all staff to observe and be observed for one hour per term). The feedback sessions to be observed by team leader or deputy team leader ■ Use of video camera, purchase of tape	■ £10 ■ Supply costs ■ Tape £10	■ Coaching training for deputy team leader 2 hours ■ Supply costs	■ TEAM LEADER/ DEPUTY TEAM LEADER	■ Published list of at least 12 activities for Years 7–10. ■ Each teacher to have been observed for at least 30 minutes during the year ■ Each teacher to have observed another teacher for at least 30 minutes and have given feedback. Each observer to have received feedback on the quality of their observation and feedback. ■ Deputy team leader and team leader to deliver appropriate advice and feedback on observation. The quality of feedback to be consistent. ■ At least three lessons to have been videotaped and discussed. ■ Issues affecting pace to have been discussed at least three times during the year.

TABLE 4.10 Continued

IMPROVEMENT 3 Year 10/11 Ma1 Assessment – some students are being piloted with coursework at GCSE, others are being prepared for the Terminal Test.	■ Evaluate the pilot – in 2001 by team leader/Mr Hodson, in 2002 by team leader/Mrs Handy. ■ Develop a flexible pro-gramme, which responds to the needs of the students and the skills of the teacher – i.e. allows teachers to choose either the coursework or Terminal task programme.	■ Photo-copying ■ Strategies time	■ Day at Linkside during June/July 2001 ■ Use of Strategies and Freed Time	■ Supply costs	■ Team leader (Coursework) and deputy team leader (Terminal Task)	■ Pilot scheme evaluated. Results of Coursework groups to be at least comparable with results from 1999 (the year before the syllabus change) and/or at least 10% higher than marks from 2000 ■ Each Coursework/Terminal Task to have a preparatory unit to be followed by the task itself. There will be at least five such units of work
IMPROVEMENT 4 ICT at KS3 and KS4 – all students follow a programme at KS3, the work at KS4 is sparse and reflects the interests and expertise of the teacher.	■ Review the KS3 programme and make the necessary changes. ■ Develop a series of activities to enhance the Mathematics curriculum at KS4 – the activities may complement Improvement 3.	■ Use of Freed Time in June/July ■ Photo-copying of materials	■		■ Team leader/deputy team leader/Mr Ball	■ Review of KS3 Units to have been undertaken and evidence of changes made if necessary. ■ Develop and trial at least one new unit of work for KS4. ■ All students to have received ICT teaching in Year 10. ■ Contribution to whole school ICT to be logged and documented by the ICT Coordinator.

TABLE 4.10 Continued

IMPROVEMENT 5						
Accelerated Learning Programme – there are eight children in Year 8 following an accelerated Mathematics programme	■ Review progress of these children. ■ Identify children in current Year 7 to begin the programme. ■ Debate the long-term programme for accelerated pupils. ■ Accelerated programme children to have one lesson per week taught in a small group.	■ Two extra timetable periods for staff to teach the pupils.	Cost of two extra periods on the time-table.	INSET – depending on staff involved and additional book resources (10 × £12)	£120	All	■ Year 7 pupils identified by March 2001 and working on Year 8 materials until the end of Year 7 and beginning Year 9 programme in September 2001. ■ Current Year 8 pupils (1999 entry) to complete Year 10 material by the end of Year 9. ■ We will have considered entering Current Year 8 (1999 entry) accelerated students for Extension Paper at KS3 and GCSE in Year 10. ■ Lesson plans for small group lessons to be published. ■ Policy written which states explicitly the aims, objectives and resources for Accelerated Learning Programme.

TABLE 4.10 Continued

IMPROVEMENT 6			
Raising pupil attainment at KS3 and KS4.	■ Targets to be set for each pupil in Year 10 and 11 (see enclosed document). ■ The targets will be reviewed at calendar points. ■ Actions include letters to parents, discussion with staff, discussion with pupils. ■ Strategies to include Improvements 2, 3 and 4 at KS4 in addition to the programme of Terminal Tasks and Revision Classes.	■ Costs included in previous Improvement details.	Team leader and Department	■ Target documents and reviews completed. ■ Action taken and documented. ■ Targets reached and evaluation of Target Setting undertaken.

TABLE 4.11 Addressing targets through an improvement plan

Target	Response
Curriculum – continue to target INSET, departmental and year team time to strategies to improve teaching and learning. Encourage a range of teaching styles. Create more opportunities for staff to communicate good practice.	Improvements 1, 2, 3, 4, 5
Raising pupil achievement	Improvements 2, 3, 6
Curriculum enhancement – provide support for high ability pupils. Each Department to have at least three clear and distinct strategies for providing opportunities for able children to be stretched beyond what is offered in the normal curriculum.	Improvement 5
Ofsted issues ■ Improving the quality of teaching and learning at KS3	Improvements 1, 2, 3, 4, 5
■ Poor lesson planning resulting in ineffective teaching	Improvement 2
■ Taking account of prior achievement from KS2 to KS3	Improvements 1, 2
■ Developing algebraic skills earlier	Improvements 1, 2
Target setting	Improvement 6

Making sure the development plan is carried out

Having spent a long period of time working with the team to construct the development plan and securing the support of the senior management team of the school, your task now is to ensure that it gets implemented.

This is essentially project management, a process we looked at in some detail earlier, see pages 17–19. For you as middle manager the issues are:

- Who is going to carry out the various aspects of the plan? Someone may be very keen but not have the right skills and experience yet to take on the task. How will you handle that?
- What support do you need to give?
- At what stages do you need progress reports?

It is of vital importance to have effective systems for development planning and ensuring that the initiatives you introduce are brought about in a coherent manner. How you choose to monitor this development will depend a good deal on the nature of the task, the relationships in the team, and the culture of the organisation and the size of the team. In a small team, where people work closely together, the monitoring can be daily and fairly informal. However, if you are leading a large team, perhaps in a split-site school, you will need more formal methods for ensuring that tasks are completed. This is part of the contracting process and one way to monitor the work is to use a diary to remind yourself of meetings and the work which needs to precede the meeting.

If development planning is to be successful and not a rod which you use to beat yourself with, it has to be planned and tenaciously managed. This is not to say it is rigid. Things change. However, by planning and anticipating change, this becomes less of an issue. There will be staff who are hostile to the changes you are trying to bring about. You must ensure that the process of change means that all the teachers have to comply with the development. Dealing with the objections raised by a hostile or obstinate teacher is not easy and you should not expect to do this alone. However, by planning a system which requires participation and is monitored carefully, objections can be managed. You need to engage the support of the team by thorough planned delegation and the support of the senior management team by updating them on the work. Where there is still difficulty, you can appeal to the work of the team and the leaders of the school for support.

_____ Summary _____

Our intention is that, at the end of this chapter, you will have:

- considered the nature of leadership and management
- looked at some models of management and considered how they apply to you

- considered the need for a planned curriculum
- developed a vision for your role and considered how to share the vision with the team
- become aware of the variety of responses that can emerge during change and how to deal with them
- appreciated the need for development planning and considered how to incorporate monitoring into the planning cycle.

chapter five

Links with senior staff and peers

Line management

Being managed

Appraisal

Administrative control

Team reports

Summary

Appendix – an Annual Report

Chapter 4 discussed the ways in which middle managers could effect a vision for their role. The importance of this overview is rarely overstated because it determines the direction in which the team will move and, with effective management, the progress that the team is able to make.

Schools are characterised by their hierarchies. Perkin (1969) has suggested that in England in the nineteenth century the rapidly expanding middle classes were the 'pugnacious protagonists of the ideology of free and open competition, epitomised by examinations'. In the nineteenth century public schooling was recounted as being a life of order, regularity and serious purpose in religion, study and games (Heward (1984)). Schools were organised into finely graded hierarchies, pupils were ranked by form. Between the Wars there was an increase in the central control of the many examination bodies which had grown up piecemeal in the nineteenth century. The gradual reform and introduction of statutory control in different professions since 1850 ensured that by 1930 most had minimum ages and educational qualifications for entry and a considerable training period. Training varied from the lengthy part-time training in banking and accountancy to five years' university education needed in medicine. In some professions promotion also depended on further examination success. A number of professions were organised in a hierarchy of seniority, with an associated ladder of promotion for the ambitious to scale, from curate to archbishop, for example. Heward (1984) describes how the bureaucratisation and professional-isation of the leading professions led to the notion of a career as a systematic preparation and training followed by regular progress to a senior position in an established and respected occupation. Attempts to impose business models on schools have, in many ways, emphasised the hierarchical structures, which are traditional and have been the cause of much difficulty. In the past teachers were led by a headteacher or chief master – or whatever title had been given to them. As the job became more complicated there developed the jobs of heads of subjects, deputy head teachers and the like. The introduction of promoted posts such as year heads, deputy year heads, phase coordinators, etc., is comparatively recent and underlines the complexity of the leadership and management role.

In many schools, teachers have multiple roles. In most primary schools the deputy head is also a class teacher. In secondary schools, the subject head will be a class teacher and usually a pastoral tutor as well. In this context the subject head is a manager and leader to his/her team and an integral part of the teaching team, but is also subject to the line management of a pastoral head (such as head of year, head of upper school, etc.). In addition, this person is also line-managed by, perhaps, a deputy head and is ultimately accountable to the headteacher. In many ways this is what makes school management complex – people are both managers and managed – leaders and led. Taken to conclusion, the class teacher is a manager of learning and has that role for all his/her classes. This aspect of school leadership has to be borne in mind when considering the stance to take when line managing your team and also, when meeting with your own line manager.

In this chapter we discuss this aspect of the middle manager's role and this will be based around the following topics:

- how to line manage your team and be line managed
- appraisal
- performance management
- budget control
- stock control
- preparing reports on the work of the team.

Line management

Line management is testing and has to be practised in order to be undertaken successfully. It requires clarity of thought and some precision. In some situations it will require tenacity and determination and such instances will be discussed in greater detail later in this section.

TABLE 5.1 Line management

- start with a clear job description
- make the expectations clear

- establish a clear contract
- establish lines of communication
- keep accurate records
- celebrate success and respond to difficulties early on.

There are a number of aspects of line management which should be in place:

- policies
- procedures
- communication
- reporting.

You should first ensure that there are policies which detail the remit of the team. For a subject leader or curriculum coordinator these will include policies on:

1. marking and assessment
2. use of ICT in the subject
3. cross-curricular initiatives
4. aims of the subject
5. spiritual, moral, cultural and personal development
6. staff development policy
7. equal opportunities policy.

The importance of these policies is that they describe the work of the team and explain how these issues are to be addressed throughout the work of the team. In all cases, such policies should be in line with the whole school policies; however, there will be subject specific areas that require closer definition, as this first case study illustrates.

CASE STUDY

Joanne

Joanne is Maths coordinator at Laney Primary School. The recent Key Stage 2 Maths results are satisfactory but have not risen in line with Joanne's predictions. Joanne has worked with all the teachers to develop a scheme of work which details the content for each unit of work, and the Numeracy hour is progressing nicely.

> Joanne looks through all the test papers and sees that there are a number of areas of weakness in Year 6. She arranges a meeting with the headteacher to discuss her plans for the next year.

This is a familiar situation for many of those in the middle management role. There are schemes of work that detail the content of lessons and there are resources to support this work. There are a number of issues which arise in this case study. One of these is the Numeracy Hour. This is a Government initiative; the school has no choice but to introduce and deliver the programme to the children. However, the tasks for Joanne are:

1 To ensure that the Numeracy hour is being delivered.

2 To ensure that the scheme of work is being followed.

3 To ensure that standards of attainment are raised.

Schemes of work can only take a group so far. By setting out dates, themes, content, resources, etc., the middle manager can do much to improve the curriculum that is offered to children and delivered by teachers. However, in order that the scheme of work is maximised there are a number of steps which need to be taken and these will be discussed in detail.

TABLE 5.2 Stages Joanne needs to follow

Stages

1 Construct a monitoring system to support the scheme of work.

2 Communicate the system to those in the team and to the line manager.

3 Develop the schemes of work through a programme.

4 Use the principle of assessment and the aims of target setting to rise standards.

Monitoring

Earlier we described the complexity of the middle management function and related this to the multiplicity of roles undertaken by the postholder. It is essential to develop systems which do not place an unreasonable burden on you – you still have your own classes to teach and the importance of this is clear. To be a successful middle manager, you need to be an excellent classroom practitioner.

Middle managers need to develop their professional competence to the highest standards. This is, in our view, fundamental to effective leadership. The best middle managers are also the best teachers because they are able to develop their remit with the commitment to the classroom at the fore. All systems and procedures should work to promote and facilitate the highest classroom standards. They should not detract from this. Developing strong classroom skills that promote and maximise learning is a lifelong challenge and is the core purpose of anyone teaching in a school.

Therefore, systems need to be in place to enable you to focus on the purpose of monitoring. Otherwise they are onerous and occasionally futile. Monitoring, at a functional level, is about ensuring that the curriculum is being delivered – that things are being done. If that is all that happens (and that might be a big step in some organisations) it misses an opportunity to undertake the analysis to facilitate quality assurance (the analytical level).

TASK 23

Analytical and functional monitoring

This task asks you to consider these two levels of monitoring and how you as a middle manager might monitor the work of a team.

Table 5.3 lists the activities that are undertaken by teachers at Joanne's school (from the case study on pages 140–1). Complete the table indicating first how Joanne can ensure that the work is done (i.e. at the functional level) and how she can monitor at an analytical level.

There is space in the table for you to include other issues pertinent to your role.

TABLE 5.3 Teacher activities at Joanne's school

Element from the scheme of work	Monitoring at the functional level	Monitoring at the analytical level
1. Pupils will work through the exercises in the text book resource.	<ul><li>Regular scrutiny of teachers' records</li><li>Regular scrutiny of pupils' exercise books</li><li>Monitoring of mark books</li><li>Classroom observation – comparing lesson</li></ul>	<ul><li>Qualitative analysis of work produced by pupils</li><li>Regular discussion of pupils' progress</li><li>Progress checks</li></ul>

Element from the scheme of work	Monitoring at the functional level	Monitoring at the analytical level
	notes with expected stage	
	■	
	■	
2. Pupils will conduct a survey and produce a wall display.	■	■
3. Pupils will use their survey to produce graphs using EXCEL.	■ Produce a rota for pupils to receive teaching on EXCEL	■
	■	
	■	
4. Pupils will complete unit tests on each topic.	■	■ Set targets and compare progress ■ Receive progress reports ■ Pupils produce subject reviews
5. Pupils will do investigations.	■	■
6. Pupils will learn to create a spreadsheet.	■	■
	■	■
	■	
	■	
	■	■
	■	■
	■	■

There are a number of ways in which monitoring at a functional level can be undertaken:

■ Produce a timetable (for example, to use ICT facilities, use the sports equipment, etc.)

- Incorporate the use of specialist equipment or particular units of work into the scheme of work.

- Make the use of the equipment or the delivery of a new unit of work part of the assessment process (i.e. the assessment of pupils cannot be completed without delivering the unit of work).

- Link units of work together.

- Develop common systems for record-keeping so that the records fall into particular categories – this will emphasise the need to complete the work.

- Informal discussion.

- On student reviews, ask questions that require students to comment on all the differing aspects of the work.

This list is endless – the important feature of all the above suggestions is that they rely on the teacher to deliver the work and not on the middle manager to engage in a long process of checking. To check that every student has done a piece of work – perhaps using Desk Top Publishing – will take a great deal of time – it is far better for middle managers to spend their time undertaking analytical monitoring. This will improve the quality of teaching and learning and be more effective in the development of the subject or curriculum area.

Analytical monitoring is by its very nature more effective, because it requires the teacher and middle manager to engage in some kind of dialogue based around the student's work. It has a number of stages:

1 *Quantitative* – this may be relevant here. For example, in some areas the amount of work produced is significant. Whilst few would argue that quantity is any kind of substitute for quality (and this is not our view) certain curriculum areas will need to make some kind of judgement. Clearly, students will not make good progress if they are not doing much work! However, there is a balance – lots of work at the same level is worse! The middle manager has to assess how the quantity of work compares with expected norms.

2 *Level of work* – is the level of work appropriate? Is the work produced at the expected level? If the students are making good progress at the levels indicated by the schemes of work, the middle manager can be satisfied with the work being done. However, the middle manager may need to make an assessment and judge the levels accordingly.

3 *Qualitative* – this kind of judgement varies according to the remit of the team. The middle manager can make links to target setting. The middle manager will need to assess the quality of work and the level at which each individual student is working. Qualitative monitoring is about reviewing what each student is doing – it is vital to undertake this process in the context of a full review. (It does take quite a time to do because it involves considering the target levels and assessing progress against these targets.) However, the resulting analysis will inform the middle manager about the progress being made by the class and will facilitate a focused discussion on the salient points.

4 *Evaluative* – as part of a team review, the middle manager might evaluate the work produced and could involve the teacher in the process. In this context, monitoring becomes a dynamic process; the teacher uses the work of his/her class to communicate with the middle manager. Together they discuss the work of the students and use this to set targets for the work of the individual students.

Many middle managers will wish to undertake the analytical monitoring processes. However, if the work of the team is at a fairly early stage, functional monitoring is appropriate. You need to take a long-term view on this if you are to bring about long-lasting change which makes a difference to students' attainments. Planning the nature of monitoring as part of the development process will enable you and the team to measure progress.

Some of the outcomes from the monitoring process will tell you about the team's capability; you need to handle such data with sensitivity but also a measure of detachment. It is important that you learn to separate collegial loyalty with the demands of your role and the responsibility you have; this is not an easy transition to make as the next case study illustrates.

CASE STUDY

Results of monitoring

Joanne has set up a system for monitoring the Numeracy hour delivery. She arranges to sample the books from all classes to review the progress being made on the plans to improve the teaching of Shape. She samples five books from each class. The unit of work the Year 6 teacher prepared on Patterns in Polygons has been done in a very cursory manner. The work produced by the children is poorly done and there are some incorrect references. The other topics have been done to a satisfactory standard.

Joanne is line manager to the Year 6 teacher. What actions should she take?

This scenario is not uncommon for middle managers because it illustrates the integral nature of school management systems. School management depends heavily on cooperation simply because teachers have a high level of autonomy in their classrooms, and this is emphasised by the isolated nature of the teaching task.

There are a number of questions that Joanne will need to ask:

1 *How was the unit of work created?* Teachers in middle management roles will often create units of work for pupils to address certain issues and to meet specific objectives. However, ways need to be found to engage all the users in this creative process. Possibilities include sharing pieces of work as they are created and dividing up the unit of work so that all the users will contribute to the whole piece. Otherwise, the opportunity to review the unit of work needs to be made during a meeting time; putting such an item on an agenda, creates a climate for sharing and collaboration. It also means objections and difficulties can be managed appropriately. Successful implementation of measures depends not only on the quality of work undertaken, but also on the strategies Joanne uses to introduce her solution. In addition, any training necessitated by a new initiative needs to be built into the lead-time before a project comes on line.

2 *What are the assessment objectives and do they match the required outcomes?* In any curriculum plan, the assessment needs to be integrated into the tasks. To do otherwise is to create a monster – the curriculum is sufficiently full in itself – ways need to be found to build the assessment tasks into the unit of work. The range of assessment opportunities has to be mapped out across the curriculum; otherwise it is piece-meal and lacks coherence. The assessment objectives should be made clear at the start of the unit of work – this has the effect of raising the profile of the assessment process. If ways can be found to incorporate pupil or student assessment into the task then so much the better. For example, a unit of work in a foreign language might have the following objectives:

By the end of the unit of work on Drinks, the student will:

- Know the words in French for a range of beverages
- Be able to spell the words accurately
- Have participated in role-plays to purchase a drink in a café
- Have written a conversation between a café owner and a person ordering drinks

---

Such objectives might be assessed using tests, oral assessment and assessment of written work. However, by informing pupils of the assessment objectives, they could assess their own progress at the end of the time period. By linking teaching, pupil assessment and teacher assessment together – perhaps in some kind of grid in a pupil's folder – the need for the teacher to undertake his/her tasks is emphasised. Few teachers can ignore the pupils who insist on the work being done to fulfil their learning objectives (and enable them to fill in their grids)!

3 *Does the teacher have sufficient knowledge to deliver the unit of work?* This is where the work becomes difficult. A sensitive middle manager will know the profile of the team and anticipate the training needs of the teachers. However, the reluctance which an experienced teacher (particularly one in a promoted post) will demonstrate cannot be underestimated. There are teachers who, like many other people, will become adept at disguising their lack of knowledge. Joanne can approach this issue by providing guidance which spells out the knowledge required. Joanne might discuss the matter with the teacher; it may be appropriate for her and the teacher to plan and rehearse the lesson or she might deliver a sample lesson as part of a training session or arrange for the teacher to observe her delivering the unit of work. However she tackles this issue, the responsibility for addressing the problem is hers; the pupils need to be taught by a person secure in their knowledge of the subject. It is incumbent on Joanne to ensure that this is the case and to make appropriate arrangements otherwise.

4 *What is the problem?* The problem may have been a local issue – there may have been circumstances about which Joanne is unaware which prevented the class teacher from delivering the unit of work at the specified time. This needs to be discussed openly and Joanne and the teacher should then agree on a programme to address any deficiencies caused by this lapse in standards. At this stage, having agreed a programme, Joanne has to make it clear how she will monitor the remedial work; it might be appropriate to see all of the books from the class to ensure the tasks are complete.

It is possible that in the course of such a discussion, a wide range of issues might emerge. These can range from issues to do with personal organisation to disaffection to obstinacy. Joanne needs to anticipate these possible reactions and respond accordingly. However, her responses will be easier if there has been transparency and clarity of purpose; subterfuge and manipulation are rarely successful in the long term. It is our view that it is always good advice to act with integrity and honesty. There may be difficulties – but manipulating people or the facts does not ease these; they certainly do not engender respect. Taking on colleagues is never easy; however, the ability to 'move teachers on' – whether this means from incompetence to dismissal, poor performance to satisfactory performance or very good to excellence – is the hallmark of a highly effective middle manager.

To summarise at this stage there are a number of features of the monitoring process which need to be considered:

TABLE 5.4 Characteristics of effective monitoring

Effective and efficient monitoring is characterised by:

- Careful analysis of the needs of the students

- Planning to address student need

- Using Assessment opportunities to inform planning

- Integrating Assessment processes into the teaching programme

- Exploring opportunities for Student Self-Assessment

- Using the creative stages of units of work a development tool

- Making the monitoring aspect explicit to students and their teachers

- Carrying out the monitoring is planned and equitable manner and responding to the issues as they arise

- Keeping records of the stages in the process and the outcomes

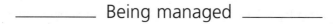

Being managed

The previous section dealt with how to approach the line management of staff to ensure that the functional aspects of the job are delivered appropriately. The middle manager is not the end of the line, however. You are responsible to your line manager who might be the deputy head or the headteacher depending on the size of the school and the nature of the role. The way in which you approach your own responsibilities for accountability is an important aspect of your work.

The situational aspect of the job is clearly fundamental to this debate. In a small school where there are close working relationships, conversations will be dominant and there is scope for regular reports to the line manager. In a large school, however, interactions with the line manager may be infrequent. One can envisage in a split-site school, a face-to-face conversation occurring perhaps weekly. Whatever the situation, there are a number of considerations for the middle manager.

The need to know. In the early stages of a relationship there is considerable value in the middle manager advising his/her line manager of all activity. This will give the line manager confidence in the middle manager's ability to discharge his/her duties efficiently and effectively. As time goes on the middle manager's confidence grows and with it the line manager's confidence in the middle manager there will be less need to inform on everything.

There are some items of information which we would suggest are relayed as a minimum:

- meeting agendas
- minutes of meetings
- development plans
- job descriptions
- letters to parents and to other agencies
- memoranda to the whole team
- budget statements
- issues which might be the precursor to disciplinary procedures.

Being line-managed is about ensuring that your line manager is clear about the work that you are doing. By keeping your line manager supplied with information and progress reports, they can support you in what you do.

TABLE 5.5 Being line-managed

- copy-in your line manager when you write memoranda
- discuss potential difficulties (particularly those concerning appraisal and performance management)
- discuss planning development activities with your line manager to gain support
- use your line manager as a 'critical friend' when planning new ideas and controversial initiatives
- keep accurate records of the meetings you have

Appraisal

The subject of appraisal has been a source of political and professional difficulty for many years. However, the Technical Paper on Teachers' Pay and Conditions gives some important insights into the ways in which the matter is likely to develop.

Effective appraisal needs to be embedded into the professional management of staff. To limit any appraisal system to an assessment of the teacher's performance in the classroom is to neglect the wider role that many teachers have – particularly in the case of middle managers. The legislated purpose of appraisal is to assist school teachers in their professional development and career planning and decision makers in their management of school teachers to promote the quality of education through assisting teachers to realise their potential and carry out their duties more effectively.

It is important to state, at this early stage, that appraisal may not be used as a disciplinary sanction. Gold and Szemerenyi (1997) set out the objectives that any appraisal system should represent:

TABLE 5.6   Gold and Szemerenyi's appraisal system objectives

- To recognise the achievements of teachers and help identify ways of improving their skills and performance.

- To assist teachers, the governing body and (where relevant) the LEA in determining whether a change of duties would help professional development and career prospects.

- To identify potential for career development supported by in-service training.

- To assist teachers experiencing difficulties by offering guidance, training and counselling.

- To inform those responsible for providing references.

- To improve the management of schools.

However, whilst the subject of appraisal is still being debated and the final procedures subject to agreement and implementation, there are a number of issues which middle managers should consider:

- What is the function of appraisal?

- What information is required?

- How should data be collected?

- How should the process be managed?

- How should difficult issues be tackled?

- How can targets be set to facilitate professional development?

- What do I do if it goes wrong?

The next part of this section deals with each of these issues in turn.

What is the function of appraisal?

The principle of appraisal is that it should be a summative statement of the teacher's performance as a professional. It should not, therefore, be restricted to a set of statements about the teacher's classroom performance – for middle managers in particular there are potential dangers in this narrow perspective. Although we would argue that the most important role for middle managers is excellence in the classroom, the function of middle managers is far wider than that.

It is important that the middle manager is an excellent classroom practitioner. His/her role is to guide the team towards improved classroom skill and the middle manager needs to be able to demonstrate those practices himself/herself. In some ways, this illustrates the complex nature of middle management in schools – of which much has been said already – that the middle manager is the leader and manager of a team, but also has a full teaching load as well. It is difficult to avoid clichés when describing this state – but being able to 'hack it' in the classroom is of fundamental importance in establishing and maintaining credibility within the school in general and the team in particular. This is why you need to ensure that the standards you set are practised in your own classroom; to do otherwise leaves you open to at best challenge, at worst ridicule.

The appraisal process, therefore, we suggest, should encompass all aspects of the teacher's work and, for the middle manager, reflect the role the middle manager has. There are many ways in which this can be managed and local agreement and proforma may specify the procedures. However, there is scope for the middle manager to define the parameters of the appraisal process, but this needs to be debated with the senior management team in the school.

A good place to start, however, is with the job description. This statement is contractual and it provides a basis against which the teacher's performance can be assessed. A good job description includes not only the task of teaching classes, but also those additional responsibilities which the teacher has as part of his/her remit. Thus, by looking at the performance of the teacher against these specifications, the appraiser has a sound and non-contentious basis on which to begin.

One way of managing this is to develop an appraisal preparation process. This process has distinct stages.

1 The appraiser gives the appraisee a copy of the job description. Both parties assess the appraisee's performance as *successful* (with supporting evidence), *needing development* (a competence which is in need of development) or *unsure* (when it cannot be stated with clarity, or there is insufficient evidence to support either view). By assessing each of the areas in terms of a competence rating, the agenda for the appraisal process becomes clear. Where there is agreement on the areas and both parties agree the work is successful, there is the opportunity for praise and the appraisal has already achieved a positive outcome. Where both rate performance as needing development, there can be an assessment of the progress already made and a programme of support can be agreed. Where either party is unsure, again, the matter can be debated or evidence cited to support the assertion.

Where parties disagree the issue needs to be discussed, but the primary outcome of this first stage is that the focus for the appraisal is clear. If there is disagreement, the appraiser and appraisee need to be able to cite evidence to plead a case: there has to be a caveat in all performance management systems that where there is major irreconcilable disagreement, the assertion of the appraiser forms the appraisal statement, but that the appraisee has the right to record his/her disagreement and this note is included in the record.

However, this matter does raise an important question regarding the function of the appraisal process. It should not, in our view, be a mechanistic process where the two parties wait to tell one another what they think; to this end, the process should be summative. If the appraisal process is used for the middle manager to express disquiet about the teacher's work – it is an abuse of the process. Similarly, if the procedure is the only time when a teacher's work is recognised positively, it is poor management. An effective appraisal should not produce surprises; it should be an honest summative statement which details the teacher's successes and performance measured against the criteria set down. It needs to be formative because, without outcomes, it lacks any kind of 'teeth' and can become a cosy nebulous chat with little to benefit either party.

Collecting data

A variety of information can be used to carry out a performance assessment of a teacher. However, in order to make the process fair and open, you should consider what type of information you are going to collect. In Task 24 you will be asked to consider this issue and think about what information is best to collect to answer particular questions.

TASK 24

Collecting information for performance appraisal

There are different types of information and data that will be required for an appraisal interview. Some of these will be qualitative, quantitative and others factual, some attitudinal. Use Table 5.7 below to consider:

What kind of performance would lead to these issues being raised?

What kind of evidence could be collected?

TABLE 5.7 Performance indicators and evidence

Teacher performance indicator	Exemplar performance characteristics	Type of evidence
Quality of teaching	■ Lessons are of an excellent standard. ■ Teaching has clear intentions. ■ Teaching is well organised. ■ Teaching has well-defined outcomes. ■ ■ ■	■
Effectiveness of teaching	■ Teaching adds value to students' outcomes. ■ Teaching is focused. ■ Results. ■ ■	■
Management of staff	■	■
Quality of teaching resources	■	■
Contribution to work of the team	■	■

Relationships with students ■   ■

Relationships with team   ■   ■
members

Relationships with parents ■   ■ Observation of teacher
                                                   at parents' consultations.
                                                 ■ Letters received by
                                                   teacher and about
                                                   the teacher.
                                                 ■

                                                 ■

                                                 ■

                                                 ■

                                                 ■

This analysis is necessary because it helps to clarify what you are trying to do when you are collecting data for the appraisal interview. It is easy to set down a brief for the data collection which is too wide-reaching and too vague. By concentrating on the specific issues which arise from the initial appraisal interview, the need for information becomes clear.

You should consider how you intend to collect the data that you need. Different ways of doing this are listed in Table 5.8.

TABLE 5.8 Data collection

Type of data	Method of collection
Quantitative data	This type of data is needed when measuring the performance of the teacher against specific targets, e.g. the teacher's ability to add value to the cognitive ability targets set by the school. To do this you would need to have a list of some of the targets (e.g. the Key Stage 3 targets for the class) and compare these with the actual results. In this way you can create useful data on which to carry out the appraisal process. Other examples might

be the number of homework tasks set and assessed recruitment to courses for which the teacher has particular responsibility and the like.

Qualitative data	This type of data is very important when considering the quality of the relationships within the team. For example, you and the teacher may choose to carry out some kind of attitudinal survey among the students to assess the attitude to the subject, the confidence they have in their teacher and so on. Such a survey is not to be undertaken lightly; however, where this process is managed sensitively, it can produce useful information which both parties can consider in depth.
Assessing teacher outputs	A good deal of valuable information can be gleaned from examining the outputs from the teacher's work. For example, the examination of the worksheets produced by the teacher will give a valuable insight into the level of work set for classes, the standard of presentation, the amount of work set for students, etc. This kind of data is useful when considered with attitudinal survey results and the effectiveness of the teaching assessment.
Classroom observation of teaching performance	This aspect of the teacher's work is the most important for all the obvious reasons. Without effective teaching, the teacher is failing. The monitoring process will be used to measure the performance of teachers throughout the year, but the appraisal process is useful in defining the state of a classroom teacher's work at the given time. The appraisal can be of particular use here, but it should not be seen as an opportunity to tell the teacher facts about his/her teaching that have been evident throughout the year – it is unfair to do so.

Tackling difficult issues

Tackling difficult issues that arise from the appraisal process is, in some ways, no different from the approach taken at any other time. However, the increasing importance of appraisal and performance management in relation to pay and advancement means that you have to be certain that your procedures are fair and that you can substantiate your judgements with evidence.

In the previous section, we discussed the need to acquire quality data in an open manner. By agreeing the type of evidence that you will collect and the means by which you will do so, you are giving the teacher the opportunity to register any disquiet with the proposals. If the teacher disputes the necessity of the data collection you have a number of choices:

1 To continue to negotiate with the teacher until agreement has been reached. This clearly has a number of advantages; not least the teacher is able to see that you take the objections seriously. However, you need to prepare the case thoroughly and be confident in your assertion of the appraisal process. Put simply, the disagreement at the initial stage is resolved most effectively by both parties agreeing to disagree, but both being required to produce evidence to support their cause.

2 To seek clarification with your line manager. This can be particularly useful if you are not used to carrying out appraisal. Indeed, anyone new to this aspect of the middle management role is advised to take advice from the management team in the school. It is important to be fully conversant with the procedures and aware of the implications and potential outcomes of your actions. The appraisal process is not a disciplinary process and there needs to be no ambiguity about your role at this stage. When preparing to do an appraisal, you should raise the prospect of any difficulty with a senior manager and discuss the actions and outcomes in detail. This way, you can be secure in the steps you take when managing the appraisal process.

3 Asserting your view and judgement. As the line manager, you are empowered to state your professional judgement as the person responsible for the work of the team. However, appraisal is intended to be a collaborative process and the appraisee has access to, and the right to comment on, what you say. At this juncture, the process is confined to the professional ambit of the school and so the support of the headteacher is crucial when faced with difficult situations.

An important issue at this stage in this consideration of difficult issues is what happens when the appraisal process raises issues of professional competence. There are specified compulsory elements of teacher appraisal and these include:

- classroom observation
- an appraisal interview which will include setting targets

- preparation of an appraisal statement
- a formal review meeting.

However, classroom observation may indicate, for example, that a teacher has difficulty in controlling classes. The correct outcome for this in the appraisal context is training and guidance from more experienced colleagues. The question of target setting is discussed in the following section.

Setting targets

A fundamental element of teacher appraisal is the setting of targets. To give the process some coherence, we advise setting targets as a direct response to the data collection. It is important to prepare thoroughly for this aspect of the task, because in many cases, those who need the targets will be reluctant to accept the necessity of the process at all.

In Table 5.9 below, we detail several outcomes from the data collection phase and suggest targets for the teacher. A target must be measurable over time and achievable. Furthermore, the actions should support the teacher and facilitate the achievement of the target; the actions should not run counter to the targets set by the appraiser.

TABLE 5.9 Outcomes and targets

Outcome	Target and action
Disciplinary issues raised from classroom observation	- Training and guidance from colleagues - Arrangements for the teacher to observe other staff, with specific criteria for the observation - Arrangements set out to support the teacher - Discussion of strategies for dealing with disciplinary matters *Target: To improve the behaviour management in class (this may be related to particular year groups, ability ranges, etc.).*
Quality of teaching – pace in lessons	- Discussion of strategies for setting and maintaining pace - Lesson observation - INSET on lesson planning - External courses on target setting, etc. *Target: To increase the quantity and quality of work done by students in class.*

Quality of teaching – subject knowledge	▪ Identify which areas of the subject are problematic ▪ Purchase of texts to support the teacher in acquiring the knowledge ▪ Discussion with a subject adviser or expert. ▪ Discussion of lesson notes on particular topics ▪ Demonstration lessons by the middle manager *Target: To improve the subject knowledge of (for example) the Restoration/'A' Level Inorganic Chemistry/Use of Logo, etc.*
Contribution to the team effort	▪ Discussion of role of teacher as part of a team ▪ Establishing projects where the teacher works with a variety of staff, with close monitoring ▪ Monitoring of, for example, the work produced by the teacher, against the team standard *Target: To produce a unit of work with detailed lesson notes and resources for use by the team.*
Procedural issues	▪ Clear direction by the middle manager on what needs to be done ▪ Defined reporting lines ▪ Discussion of practical issues, such as classroom layout, etc. *Target: Depends on the procedural issue.*
Relationships with students	▪ Behaviour management courses ▪ The teacher might lead a team project on some aspect of this issue ▪ Improve the comments written on work and on reports (specify the type of comments that are desirable) *Target: That all reports should contain a summative statement and a positive outcome based on the formative assessment.*

One issue that does arise from appraisal is whether a teacher is competent. This question should not arise from the appraisal process itself; it should arise from normal monitoring. However, failure to meet acceptable standards may be a disciplinary matter to be dealt with under the laid-down procedures. You would need to report to your line manager on such matters. If the appraisal process goes wrong you need to take advice on how to proceed.

To summarise the appraisal process.

TABLE 5.10 Summary of the appraisal process

- Use the teacher's job description as the starting point for the review.

- Decide on the focus for the appraisal.

- Arrange and undertake the classroom observation.

- Collect other data as required.

- Prepare material for the appraisal interview.

- Anticipate any difficulties and discuss with your line manager.

- Conduct the appraisal interview and write a statement.

- If the appraisee does not agree with the statement, discuss the issues, but if they cannot be resolved, the appraisee has the right to include a statement of his/her own.

- Set targets for the following cycle and agree the support and desired outcomes.

- Communicate the outcomes to your line manager.

- Monitor the progress of the teacher.

- Where discussion takes place in relation to the targets, take notes and provide the appraisee with a copy.

Performance management

Performance management is a system designed to help schools improve by supporting and improving teachers' work, both as individuals and as teams.

At the time of writing, it is envisaged as an integral part of the culture of the school with staff being encouraged to share a commitment to continuous improvement and to celebrating mutual success.

Schools are developing written and agreeing policies so that everyone has a clear understanding of how performance management works. The consultation document by the DfEE stated that the policy should contain the following:

1 A commitment to agree, monitor and review objectives with every teacher.

2 A clear statement of where responsibilities lie.

3 An annual timetable linked to the school planning cycles and arrangements to monitor progress.

4 Standard documentation for use by all teachers at the school.

In addition the policy should:

5 Encourage teachers to share good practice.

6 Be fair and treat all teachers consistently.

7 Be simple to operate and implement.

However, it is the process of performance management that will affect middle managers, both as those who have to make judgements and as participants in the process itself.

The process of performance management is in three stages; Planning, Monitoring and Review and we address each of these in turn.

Planning

The review cycle begins with each teacher and team leader (the phrase used by the DfEE document) agreeing what the focus of the teacher's work should be during the year and the consultation document suggests starting with a clear job description. The team leader should discuss the teacher's priorities, the needs of the pupils and personal priorities. From this discussion, the teacher and manager will agree objectives for the year and identify the expectations. The final phase of the discussion is the preparation of the teacher's work and development plan. This is important, not only because it sets out the framework for the following year's review, but also because it summarises and records the outcomes of the discussion.

The middle manager's role is to ensure that the teacher understands what his/her objectives involve, is in a position to achieve them and understands how they will be reviewed. Further, the discussion needs to be managed in such a way that the issue of factors beyond the control of the teacher are explored and the effect they may have on the objectives is made explicit. It is the team leader's responsibility to ensure that the objectives relate to the school development plan. In practice this is a fairly straightforward matter to address; however, the next task is designed to help you to develop this process.

TASK 25

Linking performance targets to the school development plan

Table 5.11 below contains part of a school development plan (SDP). In Table 5.9 you are asked to consider what the performance targets would be both for you, as middle manager, and for a teacher in your team. It is important to note that the targets should be:

- clear (in that there is clarity in what is required to be achieved)

- achievable (that the teacher can meet the objectives)

- measurable (so that the teacher understands how and when they will be reviewed).

TABLE 5.11 Linking performance targets to the SDP (1)

Objective from SDP	Performance target for a middle manager	Performance target for a teacher
Marking and assessment policies to be reviewed to include target setting and review.		
Each subject team to contract to deliver one unit of work per year, assessed using ICT and subject criteria at KS3.		
Increase the number of successes in local and national competitions and participation in events.		

There are a number of ways in which middle managers can respond to their line managers in establishing the targets. Some of a school's objectives can be translated into targets that are simply outcomes, i.e. the target might be 'the marking policy will be reviewed'. However, targets under performance management should relate to the needs of the pupils. Clearly, a target that is simply outcome-based does not address this matter. Alternatively, the target might be expressed for the middle manager as:

> The Department's marking policy will be reviewed and the processes established where assessment is based on specified criteria. The team leader will monitor this new form of assessment.

The objective relating to the use of ICT could be expressed as a target for both the middle manager and the teacher in the following way:

TABLE 5.12 Linking performance targets to the SDP (2)

Objective from SDP	Performance target for middle manager	Performance target for a teacher
Each subject team to contract to deliver one unit of work per year, assessed using ICT and subject criteria at KS3.	Subject team has three units of work with teaching notes and resources. The team should deliver satisfactory lessons where the work provides pupils with the opportunity to access at least Level 5 (in Year 7), Level 6 (in Year 8) and Exceptional performance (in Year 9).	The teacher to deliver the three units of work to his/her classes and provide evidence of teaching which indicates that pupils are extending their skills to at least…..

Clearly, the matter of targets is a personal one and needs to be addressed on that level. The point here is that the targets are specific and address the school development plan. Further, although they are driven by outcomes, these are related to pupil achievement – they show how progress will be made and how higher levels (in National Curriculum terms) will be reached.

Monitoring

If the work of teachers is to lead to a raising in standards of achievement, then the team's targets need to be effectively managed. This means that you need to pay continuous attention to progress during the year and to look for ways of monitoring the work that the team has done. Although the responsibility for meeting the targets rests with the person who has accepted them, there is obviously a management issue in supporting and directing people to succeed. One of the ways in which this is realised is through classroom observation – but this needs to be done in a planned and coordinated manner. The process for the observation needs to be set out clearly so that the observer and observed know what is happening. Good practice is to prepare the team, be explicit about the purposes of observation and where it is seen as part of normal everyday life. In order to make this possible, the observations should:

1 make use of standard proformas

2 focus on areas agreed previously

3 be as normal as possible

4 be followed up with full, constructive and timely feedback.

Review

The annual review should be seen as an opportunity for the teacher and middle manager to reflect on performance. It needs to be a structured interview that recognises the achievements and acts as a forum for discussing areas of improvement and professional development. There are four elements to this review process outlined in the performance management framework:

1 Reviewing, discussing and confirming the teacher's essential tasks, objectives and standards.

2 Confirming action agreed with the teacher in informal discussions.

3 Identifying areas for development and how these will be met.

4 Recognising personal development needs.

The outcome of this review will be a statement that records the meeting and sets out the basis for future reviews.

Administrative control

Managing people is one of the major tasks of being a middle manager – it is important to make sure that the school achieves value for money for the capitation devolved to the team. The middle manager therefore needs to establish procedures for managing stock and the budget.

TABLE 5.13 Administrative control

- set out procedures for ordering books, inspection copies, equipment, etc.
- set out a way of recording issue of books to staff and students (a database is a possibility)
- keep records of monies spent on orders
- keep records for petty cash – negotiate accounting processes with school administration systems
- ensure that the records kept are full, documented and transparent

A significant aspect of the middle manager's role will be budget responsibility. This may, in the case of a large school, be several thousands of pounds to cover the needs of a large number of children. The extent to which funds are delegated to middle managers will depend on the structures in the school. Some schools have delegated funds to middle managers to include:

- purchase of stationery
- purchase of text books
- purchase of furniture
- INSET provision.

There are a number of computer packages which will keep account of the budget. They allow users to specify fields, e.g. date, supplier, order and the status of the order. Whether you choose to use such a package or keep manual records you need to consider a number of aspects of financial management.

Record keeping

At this level there is a need to keep an accurate record of items ordered and received. Most schools will have a designated person to arrange for payment. However, we advise you to keep a log of orders and monies spent so that you can easily account for the money you have been allocated.

Most teams will have a sum of money delegated to them (often called *capitation*). To avoid any difficulty, it is important to plan the expenditure over the year. Certainly you should prioritise the expenditure and keep track of the team budget. This is good practice.

The matter of petty cash is important to raise here – schools each have their own policies on petty cash and charging students for lost books, etc. It is vital that there is transparency in all financial matters. Some kind of cashbook where income received and paid out is advised.

Authority for spending

Schools are visited regularly by publishing companies and teachers will receive offers on books and equipment. Publishers will offer schools an 'inspection' copy which the school can either purchase or return. You should clarify with your team the extent to which they can do this without authority. Schools with good control systems will only authorise expenditure from a budget with the agreement of the manager. However, it is worthwhile to clarify this with the senior management team and with the teachers in the team to avoid any difficulty.

Stock control

This is a difficult area for many middle managers. It is relatively easy to manage the stock if each teacher has control over the books and equipment – for example, if the books never leave the room. However, there is usually some slippage where items do go missing and are unaccounted for. The challenge is to minimise the effect of this. By issuing books to students and giving them the responsibility for the maintenance and safe-keeping of the book, there is redress if things go awry.

———— Team reports ————

Many middle managers will be required to produce an annual report on the work of the team. It is a useful exercise for a team leader to undertake, even if this is not school practice.

In reporting the work of the team, the middle manager should outline accurately the progress that has been made in addressing the development tasks. It is a way of demonstrating commitment to the team's work as well as detailing the needs of the team. A good report will set out the progress the team has made and the work it will undertake in the future.

TABLE 5.14 The team report

The team report should contain:

- a description of the year's work
- the progress through the development plan

- the analysis of pupil progress (related, where appropriate, to Key Stage and Examination results)
- a budget statement.

There are a number of reports that a middle manager might be required to produce:

- annual report for the headteacher
- report to the Governors
- reports to other bodies, e.g. network groups, LEA-organised groups, etc.

Although in many ways the information required to produce such a report is consistent, the audience varies a good deal, and it is this aspect of the reporting process that needs further consideration.

The information required for such a report will normally be in sections as follows:

1 *Descriptive and historical*

The function of such a section is to describe the events of the year (or other time frame). It might include details such as staff changes, curriculum changes and the like. One way of approaching this aspect of a report is to use the framework shown in Table 5.15.

TASK 26

Reporting on the team's work

Use the framework below to outline the structure of your team and to describe the work of the team over the year as part of the annual report. Focus on who, what, when, where and why the events have occurred.

TABLE 5.15 A framework for the reporting of a team's work

Question to be answered	Details to be included	Your response
Who?	■ Who is the leader of the team? ■ Who are the other team members and how are they involved in the work of the team?	

Question to be answered	Details to be included	Your response
	■ What changes have there been to the team profile?	
What?	■ What were the team's development tasks for the year?	
	■ What progress has been made in addressing these targets?	
	■ What evidence can you cite to support your assertions (link your evidence to target setting)?	
	■ What projects have been undertaken by the team and what progress have staff made?	
When?	■ When did the major events occur for the team?	
	■ When was the major development work undertaken?	
Where?	■ Was all of the team's work in school?	
	■ Did you work with outside groups, e.g. as LEA working groups, network groups, etc.?	
	■ Have there been links with feeder schools or partner schools, etc.?	
Why?	■ Why did you undertake the development you have done?	

Question to be answered	Details to be included	Your response
	■ Why have you focused on these tasks? ■ Why is the rate of progress as it is, etc.?	

The objective of this section is for you to be able to represent the work of the team in a considered manner. Further it is about providing the right amount of evidence to support the assertions that are made. There is a considerable pressure on Governors and headteachers to ensure that the development plans they establish are carried out. By setting out the work of the team in this manner, you are setting out and explaining the work that has been done.

2 *Report on the performance in public examinations*

In the past, this section might have been confined to the work of middle managers in secondary schools leading teams who entered their students for public examinations. However, with baseline assessment occurring at Reception Year stage, there is a need for managers at all key stages to reference the results when test and examinations have been taken. The infants' coordinator can relate the work of the team to the baseline assessment. Further the Key Stage 1 tests are important here. However, the challenge lies in making sense of the statistics that are produced and relating them to pupil outcomes.

The middle manager with the baseline data for the pupil concerned should have a view on what the pupil can achieve at a Key Stage. This is the target setting process. By having a rigorous targets setting process, the middle manager can compare the performance of the cohort with the target results. Clearly, where the work of the team has resulted in added value, there is cause for celebration but it also raises the question: Were the targets set, sufficiently challenging? However, where the targets have not been met, the middle manager should report in detail on the aspects of the pupil's performance which have fallen below the expected levels. The report should also include an action plan which addresses the shortcomings revealed in this analysis.

At Secondary level there is a need to report on the levels at Key Stage 3, GCSE, GNVQ and Advanced Level. Where the team has set targets for the performance of individual pupils, the results should be related to the work of teachers. However, the main outcomes from this consideration, at whatever level, should be:

- an analysis of the targets set for the pupils or students
- the results achieved by the pupils or students
- a results analysis of each teacher
- an explanation which sets out why the results are as they are
- targets for the future
- the action planning which will lead to these targets being set.

In some cases there will be development tasks and INSET (IN SErvice Training) for this plan, but this needs to be explained and justified.

3 *Future development*

The team's development plan can be restated here in a summary form. The progress of the team in realising the current development plan can be added. (Many schools operate an April–March development cycle, but the time for a report may be September, to coincide with the release of Key Stage and public examination results). Again, the five-point analysis outlined in Table 5.15 is relevant here.

4 *Budget statement*

At this stage it is good practice to produce a budget statement which indicates the expenditure of the team in delivering its work. Further it gives the team leader the opportunity to set out the needs for the rest of the year.

An example of a report is included in the Appendix to this chapter.

Summary

Our intention is that, at the end of this chapter, you will have:

- considered the nature of management in schools
- defined line management
- realised the importance of policies and the features of effective communication
- considered how to monitor the work of a team
- appreciated the need for appraisal and performance management
- considered a template for a report on the team's work.

———— Appendix – an Annual Report ————

Preamble

The Department began the academic year with a number of challenges. Unfortunately, Miss Carol Smith resigned at the end of May and despite efforts to recruit a suitably qualified replacement, we were unable to make a permanent full-time appointment. Mrs Claire Davies applied for the post and she was engaged as a supply teacher to cover the extended sick leave taken by Mrs Noreen Medlicott. The remainder of the timetable was made up by non-specialists from the existing staff – notably Mr Joe Grand (whose timetable for Mathematics was increased) and Mr Jack Lee (a Physics graduate who taught RS) and Mr Michael Chewter (a Physics teacher). Mrs Medlicott was unable to return to school. This situation caused the Department to review its staffing for Year 11 classes. Mr King taught Set 1 and Mrs Flowers taught Set 3.

Set	Year 10 teacher	Year 11 teacher
1	CS	MK
2	RT	RT
3	NM (+ supply)	JL
4	ST	ST
5	JL	CD (on supply)
6	NT	NT
7	MK	JG
8	MJ	MJ

There were some notably difficult pupils in Set 3 who were the cause of some disruption and a number of strategies and sanctions were deployed. The Department was well supported by the Senior Management Team in maintaining its control over this challenging class. Over the course of the year some were excluded from school, some were excluded from Mathematics lessons for fixed periods; some pupils were placed in other classes. The Department certainly felt under strain, but it is a credit to the effective teamwork in the Department and the strong support it offers that the situation was managed to the best of our ability.

Last year, the results for Set 1 were below the standard expected and this was attributed to the poor performance of pupils on Paper 3 (the Investigations paper). In an effort to improve the results of this particular group the class produced coursework in lieu of this Paper 3. The expectations for Set 1 were not as high as normal (given their target grades both in Mathematics and in other subjects). Also, the change in mode of assessment for Ma1 necessitated new strategies for the Department. I decided to prepare my class (Set 4) for the coursework option also. This is part of a long-term strategy to develop a flexible system where different classes are prepared for the assessment options which suit their needs best. The success of this initiative will be discussed later.

Year 10 classes continued with the Key Maths scheme. The following academic year will see the entire school working thorough the Key Maths scheme. At the start of the academic year the classes were as follows:

Set	Teacher	Tier
1	ST	Higher
2	JL	Higher
3	RT	Intermediate
4	JG	Intermediate
5	CD (on supply)	Intermediate
6	NN	Foundation
7	MJ	Foundation

Again, this represents a change in that Sets 1 and 2 are being prepared for higher tiers and JL and I have been working closely preparing these pupils for the coursework option. The results, at this stage, are good and augur well.

One consequence of this change has been that where pupils have been unable to cope with the demands of higher level Mathematics then they have moved to Set 3. This has had the effect of enlarging Set 3. Also, some difficulties with Set 5 have made standards hard to maintain. The decision has been taken, therefore, that some pupils from this group will transfer to Set 4 to do Intermediate, the rest will do Foundation. It is hoped, however, that they will be able to successfully aim for Grade D at this level.

In October, the Department commenced its next set of Senior Masterclasses. The Department was delighted to welcome the following speakers:

Date	Speaker
10 October 1998	Dr Annabelle Thirsk
17 October 1998	Dr Jack Evans
7 November 1998	Professor Jocelyn Grantly
14 November 1998	Dr Gail Sothall

Several of these speakers have been to Lakeside School before and others came because of their colleagues' good reports. I am particularly grateful for the support of Mr Pafos, Mrs Flowers and Mr Tarbutt. These colleagues willingly gave up their Saturday mornings and helped to make the events successful ones.

Junior pupils followed the Masterclasses in the Spring Term by a visit to Southampton University. The Department is grateful to Dr Ann Terrie for organising the event at Southampton. The pupils were a credit to the school and we hope to continue our work in this area by developing this idea further.

Throughout the academic year the Department has been working with its partner Primary schools. This initiative began last academic year but has widened its cope considerably. The programme includes:

- regular meetings to discuss curriculum issues

- sharing of Mathematics resources

- production of resources

- development of 'Link' Project where pupils begin a piece of work at Year 6 Induction, continue it at Primary school and then complete the work in September at Lakeside School. The high level of commitment is indicative of the quality of relationships the department has developed

- target setting – some partner schools have set targets for Year 7 pupils for number and algebra. This is a pilot project and will be kept under close review

- visits by Lakeside school staff to Primary schools, using Freed Time.

A feature of the work this year has been the inclusion of agenda items suggested and led by primary colleagues. Also, the venue for the meetings has varied to include Primary schools. This is part of the strategic plan to make the Lakeside Mathematics Liaison Group (as we have named ourselves) one which depends on the group.

This is an important part of the Department's work. During the year I addressed a meeting of Primary and Secondary school representatives outlining the work we do. It is the view of the Mathematics adviser, that the Department's work is a model of good practice and this view has been promulgated. The Department's reputation has been enhanced further by its representation at National Numeracy Strategy meetings (we were the only Secondary school to attend in the area).

The Summer term is always a busy one when the Department prepares pupils for public examinations. Our programme is one where pupils practise questions from past papers. This programme is prepared by Mr Tarbutt, but is administered by Mrs Flowers. The Department is grateful to Mrs Flowers for her meticulous organisation of these resources. This year was important to the Department because there were several new qualifications which were to be assessed:

Year	
13	Further Mathematics – this included the modules P1, P2, P3, P4, M1, M2, D1 and T1. This was a new qualification for the Department.
13	Oxbridge entrance – One student applied to Oxford and another to Cambridge.
13	A Level Mathematics – P1, P2, M1, T1 – this course replaced the Pure Maths and Statistics course.
11	Sets 1 and 4 produced coursework.

The academic year ended with the appointment of Miss Maddi Cohen and Mr Joe Grand to the permanent staff of the Department.

Staff development

The Department has continued to offer in-house training for ICT and marking. The Department sets aside Strategies Meetings time to prepare staff to deliver ICT units of work. We also offer tutorials for staff and support for classes when delivering ICT.

The Department is fortunate to have two experienced A level examiners. This expertise is used to good effect to train staff to mark using conventional procedures.

The Department has continued to develop its curriculum and has undertaken a range of activities designed to improve the quality of teaching and learning. There has been a great deal of work done with JG and NN to improve the quality of teaching. This has included JG's attendance at an external course for non-specialists. This appears to have had a positive effect. It is hoped that the siting of the Department will facilitate day-to-day monitoring.

A major part of the Department's work is the preparation of students for the terminal paper or coursework. Much work has been done, but more has still to be done, to raise the standard of teaching in this important area.

A level results

Mathematics

There were some very pleasing results for these students. Joanne Lewis gained a Grade A. Two students had done Intermediate GCSE and so it was pleasing that they secured grades C and E. This combination of modules (P1, P2, M1, T1) was a new one for the Department and was aimed at those who wanted a general Mathematics course or were not studying A level Physics or who had done GCSE at Intermediate. The results are encouraging.

Mathematics: Pure with Mechanics

These are excellent results. Two students both secured A grades. It is pleasing that Rebecca Davies gained a grade D after struggling with much of the course.

Further Mathematics and Oxbridge

One student gained AA at A Level and secured his place at Oxford.

One student gained AA and his results for STEP were Maths 2 – outstanding and Maths 3 – excellent. These are superb results for a very able student.

One student gained AA for Mathematics.

The other two students gained BB and AC respectively. These are excellent grades and bear testament to the hard work these two students did, ably supported by their teachers, over the two years.

This Further Mathematics course was new for the Department and included Decision Maths.

GCSE

The results for the cohort varied and so will be taken set by set.

Set 1

This group was taken over by the teacher at the start of Year 11. It was decided to prepare these students for the coursework option and Mr King did a considerable amount of work with this group. The decision to do coursework was taken in the light of the previous year's results. The coursework marks were unchanged by EdExcel. This is very encouraging as the moderation process was clearly sound. All students bar one achieved their Estimated Grade and several students achieved grades higher than the Estimated Grades made in January 1998. The Department has decided to extend this trial and next year's Sets 1 and 2 (both doing Higher) will be prepared for the Coursework option.

Set 2

Overall the results for Set 2 were a little disappointing in the sense that too many pupils gained a Grade D – there were six. However, of these six pupils, one of whom should have been in Set 3, two were absent for a good period of time before the exams. Of the other three, two were 'at risk' in the sense that they were the weakest students in the group and one student definitely underachieved for no apparent reason. The Grade Bs were as expected.

Set 3

The teacher experienced considerable difficulty with this group. They had received a poor level of teaching in Year 10 and it was hoped that he would be able to raise their standard. However, there was a lack of desire to work, particularly among some of the boys. The teacher worked hard to ensure that those students who wanted to do well were able to do so. In every case the results obtained by the students were at least that predicted from their mock exams.

Set 4

This group was prepared for the coursework option as part of the pilot. Again, EdExcel altered none of the marks. The results for this group were very pleasing. One student gained a Grade B and 10 achieved a Grade C. I gave Grade C as a target to the entire group, partly to see what effect this would have. It had a positive effect. A significant benefit of preparing the students for the coursework option was the amount of time it allowed to concentrate on the two written papers. This helped to raise the standard. Several students were within a few marks of Grade C. As a consequence of this success, the groups preparing for Intermediate GCSE will do the coursework option.

Set 5

Despite being taught by a supply teacher for all of Year 11, this class was able to produce some reasonable results. For the most part their results were as predicted (from their January 1998 grades).

Set 6

After having spent a good deal of time working with the class teacher to improve the quality of his teaching, it is pleasing to record some good results for this group. For the most part students achieved at or above their target grades.

Set 7

These results were in line with predicted grades. However, one student gained a Grade D – a good result for this group.

Set 8

The students who passed achieved the grades expected. Although it was anticipated that two students would get an Unclassified, it is in line with the Department's policy to enter all students who have followed the full course.

The development plan

Target/initiative	Strategies	Progress to date
IMPROVEMENT 1 Standards of numeracy vary considerably when pupils enter the school. Numeracy hour begins in Primary schools in September 1999.	■ Programme of meetings on common themes with Primary school colleagues (Year 6 teachers and/or Mathematics coordinators). ■ To hold at least three meetings during the academic year. ■ Develop the 'Link' Project. ■ Lakeside School Mathematics team to develop their links with 'their' school.	■ Meetings have been held with increasing frequency and improving attendance. ■ Items are being suggested and led by Primary staff. ■ All link projects were returned. ■ Most primary schools visited at least once.
IMPROVEMENT 2 The pace of lessons is recognised in school and nationally to be a factor in determining progress.	■ To develop a series of opening/recap activities to start lessons. ■ To encourage staff to use opening activities and to see the benefits. ■ Develop the idea of a lesson format, which uses Stating activity, Development (on themed activities) and Plenary. ■ Lessons to be videotaped for discussion at Department meetings.	■ Opening/recap activities discussed and documented. ■ Benefits of such activities discussed at Department meeting and TD Day. ■ During Department monitoring the effectiveness of these activities was monitored. ■ Idea of lesson format introduced but some resistance. ■ Videotaping to be done during Autumn term.

Target/initiative	Strategies	Progress to date
IMPROVEMENT 3 Year 10/11 Ma1 Assessment – some students are being piloted with coursework at GCSE, others are being prepared for the terminal test.	■ Evaluate the pilot – in 1998 by ST/MK, in 1999 by ST/JL. ■ Develop a flexible programme, which responds to the needs of the students and the skills of the teacher, i.e. allows teachers to choose either the coursework or terminal task programme.	■ See comments on Set 1 and Set 4.
IMPROVEMENT 4 ICT at KS3 and KS4 – all student follow a programme at KS3, the work at KS4 is sparse and reflects the interests and expertise of the teacher.	■ Review the KS3 programme and make the necessary changes. ■ Develop a series of activities to enhance the Mathematics curriculum at KS4 – the activities may complement Development 3.	■ Programme reviewed and new units introduced. ■ Training will be programmed into the Autumn and Spring term meetings time.
IMPROVEMENT 5 Accelerated learning programme – there are eight children in Year 8 following an accelerated Mathematics programme.	■ Review progress of these children. ■ Identify children in current Year 7 to begin the programme. ■ Debate the long-term programme for accelerated pupils. ■ Accelerated programme children to have one lesson per week taught in a small group.	■ Three children in Year 8 are to continue the programme. ■ No funding available for extra lessons.
IMPROVEMENT 6 Raising pupil attainment at KS3 and KS4.	■ Targets to be set for each pupil in Year 10 and 11 (see enclosed document). ■ At calendar points, the targets will be reviewed.	■ Book plate amended to include the target grade. ■ Target grades reviewed at regular points during the year.

Target/initiative	Strategies	Progress to date
	■ Actions include letters to parents, discussion with staff, discussion with pupils. ■ Strategies to include Improvements 2, 3 and 4 at KS4 in addition to the programme of terminal tasks and revision classes.	

Financial statement

Below is a statement showing all of the Department's expenditure for this academic year to date.

Balance brought forward		125.87
Income:		
1998–9 ppn	4,582.00	
Sales and Lakeside Trust Grant	3,308.77	
Total income		7,890.77
Expenditure:		
Books (Note 1)	2,390.18	
Stationery	819.22	
Photocopying	494.27	
Miscellaneous (UKMT, MA, etc) (Note 2)	2,778.21	
Total expenditure		6,481.88
Balance carried forward at 23 July 1999		1,534.76

Note 1   This includes the discounts secured by me for the purchase of Key Maths text books

Note 2   The Department is a member of the Mathematics Association and participates in the UKMT Challenges

To summarise

The staffing of the Department has improved and the centralisation of the Department and its resources is welcomed. There has been improvement in the delivery of Ma1 (Using and Applying Mathematics) but this is an ongoing development area. Also, I have been encouraging staff to consider their lesson structures and to accommodate the new ideas suggested by research and the numeracy strategy.

chapter six

Recruiting and monitoring staff

Motivation

Preparing to recruit

Interview day

Conducting an interview

Recruiting a deputy
subject leader

Managing the induction of
new staff

Monitoring and evaluation

Summary

For the majority of middle managers, the issue of recruitment will occur with relative rarity. Paradoxically, a successful school may be involved in a heavy recruitment programme, because of its success. Where there is a culture of investment in people and where this is followed through with professional development, teachers will grow professionally and find promotion elsewhere. In many ways, this is a pity. There are few professions where promotion normally requires a change of environment in the way that schooling does. There is a need for educational organisations in general to adopt a positive approach towards staff development and to create opportunities within the school for promotion. Further, an element of succession planning will enable schools to manage the recruitment process in a more controlled and proactive manner. However, the development of such processes at a whole school level is beyond the remit of this book, but as this chapter unfolds, we consider the way in which this can be achieved at the team level.

The Green Paper on Teachers' Pay and Conditions is an attempt to create a structure where more people are involved in the decision-making process in the school. In addition, the Paper (and of course, its implementation) sets out to provide a means where teachers can achieve high status and relatively high pay, whilst in their current schools, but with additional responsibilities. However, this has been discussed in greater depth in Chapter 5.

This chapter is divided into a number of interrelated sections:

- how to recruit a teacher
- how to interview a teacher
- how to recruit a newly-qualified teacher
- how to recruit a deputy subject leader
- managing the induction of new staff
- monitoring the work of the staff – lesson observations.

Motivation

This chapter begins with a discussion on motivation. In order to engage in the practice of recruitment, induction and development of a teacher, you have to understand motivation. Whilst there are few ways of measuring commitment, there are antecedents of organisational commitment that can be recognised. Role conflict and ambiguity are detrimental, whilst a participative climate, teamwork, satisfaction with work and promotion are closely related to commitment.

The issue of staff recruitment has become a source of much difficulty in some curriculum areas and in certain parts of the country. In subjects such as science, mathematics and modern languages in particular, schools have experienced considerable problems when trying to recruit suitably qualified and experienced staff. In some areas, bursaries are offered to newly qualified teachers to attract them to the area – in some cases the recruitment process begins very early in the academic year (when PGCE students have barely begun their training). There are initiatives which have been designed to address these difficulties:

1 Some schools, notably independent, recruit directly from final year undergraduates. The advantage of this scheme is that students are offered paid work instead of undertaking training. The best graduates are picked off. However, whilst this book is not seeking to make a political point, and independent schools have a duty to their pupils, as does any other school, it does place State schools at a considerable disadvantage. State schools do not have the budgetary flexibility or certainty to recruit at will – the machinations of LEA-controlled budgets are such that the exact staffing need will be determined later in the year. Further, to recruit from a pool of undergraduates is to deny the value of the PGCE. By recruiting people without the background of psychology, philosophy and sociology of education is to appoint a person whose long-term career and proficiency may be compromised. Further, the PGCE course (or the B.Ed.) gives students the opportunity to develop pedagogy related to their subject in particular and to the work of schools as a whole. In our view, to do otherwise is to be narrow and functionalist. Teaching needs rounded individuals with a holistic approach to education.

2 Subject-related bursaries for the PGCE – the 'golden hello'. These have been offered to students embarking on PGCE courses in subjects such as mathematics and science. The advantage of this initiative has been to direct the funding to the source of the problem – the lack of specialist teachers.

However, whilst the initiative has resulted in some increase in teachers for these subjects, it is the long-term career structure that has still to be remedied.

It is important to spend time reflecting on motives for joining the profession and remaining within it. The analysis of motives is important at this stage because it provides you with a theory, which underpins the questions asked and the way in which the induction process is managed. Furukawa (1982) outlines the major antecedents of motivation to work as:

■ employees' goal setting

■ employees' expectations

■ employees' cognitive evaluations.

Motivation to work is enhanced by having specified goals to work towards. In a review of the goal setting literature, Campbell (1989) concluded that both situational and personality factors affect an individual preference to work on easy or hard goals. Situational factors include such variables as prior success or failure on the task, monetary and verbal incentives, feedback, participation and competition.

The link between the previous performance and the difficulty of the goal chosen is, of course, familiar to school managers. Indeed, the process of target setting for schools has involved an evaluation of the goals the school has. Indeed, the first stage in this process is to examine the school's previous performance and to evaluate this against the background of its aims and the relative success of other schools. Further, in setting goals for itself (or agreeing the goals with the local authority) the school has to ensure that the targets set are realistic but challenging.

Put simply, we tend to choose more difficult goals if our previously assigned goals were easy and choose easier goals if our previously assigned goals were difficult.

There have been a number of studies which have examined why goal setting works at this personal level (Jackson and Zedeck, 1982; Garland 1984). The conclusion has been that jobs with clear instructions and rewards may generate goals set with more confidence, hence contribute more to task motivation than a job with ambiguous instructions and poor rewards. But the effect of the person is highly significant here. The personality factors are crucial when considering the motives a person brings to their work. The next task asks you to consider your own personal motivation and reflect on the impact this has had on your professional development.

TASK 27

Personal motivation factors

Table 6.1 below lists various factors affecting personal motivation.

Consider each one and reflect on the successes and failures you have had.

What effect have these had on your subsequent professional development?

To what extent do you set yourself goals for your professional life?

TABLE 6.1 Motivation factors

Factor	Successes	Failures	Impact
Tasks – what tasks have you undertaken?			Are you creative in your work? Are you a shaper? Are you a completer/finisher?
Monetary incentive			Is the need for increased remuneration important for you?
Verbal incentive		Have you been told about your failures in a destructive manner?	
Participation	Have you worked with others on successful projects?		
Achievement drive	What do you aim to achieve – in professional terms, in personal terms?		
Self-assurance		Have events challenged your self-assurance?	

Factor	Successes	Failures	Impact
Maturity			How have you changed over the past two years in your approach to work?

These issues are fundamental to the middle manager because without the ability to reflect on your own motives, it is difficult to be responsive to the needs of others.

There is a danger inherent in any discussion of motivation relating to the work of teachers. Much talk of motivation centres on the relatively poor levels of pay for teachers. There is, perhaps, a view that if there were more money then motivation would be increased. Whilst this may be true (and many a teacher would support the view!) it is not the end of the matter. Teachers' salaries, like those of other public sector workers will never match those in the private sector. There will always be better-paid jobs. To ignore this fact is to begin a spiral of doom which denigrates the reason why most teachers work: to teach children. To reduce the job of teaching to one which centres around money is to start a process which can never be resolved and to ignore the incentive to work which exists in most schools.

Cognitive evaluation theory has received increased attention from organisational psychologists. The impetus for concern seems to stem mainly from the practical possibility that the introduction of extrinsic rewards for behaviour may decrease intrinsic motivation rather than add to it. Put simply, by increasing the amount of money paid to teachers for their work, there is the possibility that it will decrease the intrinsic motivation – the desire to teach the subject, the desire to work with children, to create a better society, to create life chances, etc. This is because the extrinsic rewards decrease the perception of intrinsic causation: for many teachers, much of the job satisfaction they obtain comes from seeing children develop intellectually, experiencing the thrill of a child being able to perform some skill, to acquire knowledge and so on. Furukawa (1982) suggested that for extrinsic rewards to have an inhibitory effect on intrinsic motivation, the task needed to be inherently interesting, and the reward had to be administered in a contingent and salient manner under the strong situational norm of non-payment for work. It is our view that education is inherently interesting and that any attempt to reward teachers has to be seen in this light.

Preparing to recruit

The decision to recruit a teacher to the team may be taken in the light of a resignation, or a retirement, or even increasing curriculum responsibility which necessitates the enlargement of the team.

Whatever the reason, there needs to be a review of the state of the team to assess the needs of the team and to consider how it will change over the next few years. The purpose of this is to ensure that the recruitment process results in the appointment of a teacher whose skills and attributes match most closely the needs of the team.

There are several questions to consider when conducting such an audit. Table 6.2 provides a template for such a process with accompanying notes.

TABLE 6.2 Team needs audit proforma

Factor	Audit	Notes and questions
Age profile of the team		■ What is the age profile of the team? ■ What is the mean age? ■ Is the subject area seen as a 'young' subject? ■ Are there particular advances in the subject which make this an issue?
Subject expertise of the team		■ Is the team well placed for curriculum development? ■ Is there an aspect of the team's work that needs greater subject expertise (for example, is there a need for the teacher to be a scientist – so that they can act as Science coordinator).

Factor	Audit	Notes and questions
Length of service in the school		■ Clearly when recruiting from outside the school, this is less of an issue; however, the overall profile of teaching experience is relevant.
Teaching expertise in the team		■ Are there areas of teaching skill that need to be addressed? For example, is there a lack of skill in teaching particular aspects of the curriculum, e.g. delivering ICT?
Team development plan		■ How will the departure of a teacher (from the existing team) affect the plans for the future? ■ Is there a specific responsibility which needs to be undertaken?
Developments in the team's remit		■ There may be new tasks which will come 'on-line' in the near future. Is this an opportunity to appoint a person who can take these on?
Succession planning opportunities		■ By considering the profile of the team as it stands, there may be opportunities to re-shape the team and provide the scope for further development.

At the end of this audit process you will have a clear view of what kind of teacher needs to be appointed to the team. The appointment process does not, of course, take place in a vacuum. There is a need for any appointment to fit in with the needs of the school as a whole – the school may be looking for opportunities to increase the numbers of staff who can coach particular sports, or contribute to the extra-curricular life of the school – you do not have to be parochial, but have to decide what is required for the work of the team.

Before the recruitment process begins in earnest, the following items need to be in place:

- the person specification
- the job description
- the advertisement
- the details about the school
- the recruitment schedule.

Each of these is discussed in turn in the following section.

The person specification

You should be in a position to write some profile of the person that is required: a person specification. This profile sets out the kind of person that you are looking to recruit. It should be set out in the form of a list of skills and attributes that the successful appointee should possess. Examples of these are:

- a good honours graduate in....
- experience of more than one school
- a commitment to teaching junior age children
- an interest in extra-curricular activities
- a willingness to participate in the development of teaching schemes
- the ability to produce teaching resources.

In some cases it may be useful to consider what is essential and what is desirable. For example, it may be desirable to recruit a good Honours graduate in mathematics to fill a mathematics teaching post in a secondary school. However, the vagaries and uncertainties of recruitment for such posts may mean that such criteria may draw a very small field of enquiry. Therefore, to set the essential criteria as 'an Honours graduate in a mathematically-related discipline' with the 'Good Honours graduate in mathematics' as the desirable attribute may be more expedient. These are judgements you will make when consulting with the headteacher.

The objective of the person specification is to establish the kind of teacher the school is intending to appoint. It also provides the middle manager with the agenda of the recruitment process. Having composed such a document, it will drive the remainder of the process.

The job description

The next stage of the process is to determine the job description for the teacher. This should be related to the person specification and should set out in broad terms what the teacher will actually do in post. Although much of the detail that accompanies the appointment of staff to a school is beyond the remit of this book, there are certain facts which you need to know to ensure that the processes are carried out correctly. Gold and Szemerenyi (1997) write:

> 'There is no prescribed procedure for advertising posts or conducting interviews. There will usually be a job description and frequently also a person specification to ensure that the candidate who most closely meets the particular needs of the school is identified. Care must be taken to avoid discrimination, actual or perceived. It is sensible to consider all applications against a set of pre-determined criteria (which in themselves will have influenced the job description and any person description) and to have a degree of structure and some common questions to be asked at interview.'

There are a number of points to be addressed here, but at this stage it illustrates the need to have a process which is fair and does not leave the school open to charges of unfair practice. Whilst the responsibility for the process lies with the headteacher and senior staff – they will know the procedures to be followed – you should ensure that the processes that are being set out conform to the requirements laid down. Some local authorities have procedures for the process.

The job advertisement

The question of the advertisement needs to be considered. Again, some local authorities specify the format for any advertisement and there may be agreements where all advertisements for schools within an area are pooled together. However, there is normally some flexibility in the text of the advertisement. A good advertisement should contain the following information as a minimum:

- name, address and telephone number of the school
- name of headteacher
- number on roll
- type of school (e.g. boys, girls, middle, grammar, etc.)
- title of the post (including scale, CPS, etc.)
- brief details of what the post involves
- how to apply for the post – closing dates, etc.

By attending to these details, the school will save itself the time and expense of responding to unsuitable applications.

Application methods

The school will have its own methods of application – these may include application forms, CVs, letters of application and the like. There is a growing trend in asking candidates to produce a paper on a particular topic. The advantage of asking a candidate to write a paper on, for example, the impact of the National Grid for Learning on infant schools is that the selection panel may get a greater sense of what the person is about. However, this kind of exercise does increase, significantly, both the time that is spent on the selection process and the expense that is incurred. Further, the school needs to ask itself whether its processes are secure if it needs more evidence than what is normally required.

Most schools will provide candidates with further details about the school. These can take a variety of forms and can include:

- the school website
- the school prospectus
- a set of papers which includes the job description, person specification and schedule
- a paper about the team the successful candidate will be joining.

Whilst the use of the school website is becoming more popular, there is still a place for setting out in broad terms, what the team is like and how the successful candidate will fit into the team. The information collected for the audit, outlined earlier in this chapter, can be used here.

Processing applications

As the applications arrive, you will want to collaborate with the headteacher who will be longlisted. Headteachers may have particular views on the role of the middle manager in the recruitment process – this may vary from being given a shortlist just a few days before the interviews to a delegation of the entire process. However, it is reasonable to expect to be involved in the following:

- production of the advertisement
- compilation of the person specification and job description
- final shortlisting
- interviewing
- decision making.

The correct way to manage the longlisting process is to use the person specification. By constructing a grid which sets out all the criteria, it is possible to go through each application and assess it against the criteria. Some managers will use a points system for each criterion:

2 – strength

1 – some evidence

0 – no evidence.

At the end of the longlisting process there will be a rank order of candidates. The first group (say six) will be invited for interview, the remainder will be held as reserves. The advantage of this approach is that it is rigorous and fair. It means that if there is any question over the school's process, there is documentary evidence to support its methods. At this point the school may send for references.

—————— Interview day ——————

In setting up the interview day, several decisions need to be made and these will be discussed in turn.

1. Do you want the candidates to teach a class?

This practice does vary a good deal and can depend on the subject. It can be quite daunting to have to teach a class before the panel who will be interviewing for the post. However, the advantages are that the panel gets to see how the candidate relates to children at first hand. Provided that the class is well chosen and the criteria for the lesson observation is made clear, the exercise can be a valuable one. It is better, in our view, for the candidates to suffer a few 'wobbles' and discomfort than for children's education to be affected by an unsuitable teacher.

This does call into question the validity of references and the extent to which they are reliable and how accurate a picture they give of a candidate's suitability for the job. In our view, the decision to ask candidates to teach can be one the middle manager takes, but it should be in the context of a whole-school recruitment process.

There are particular instances, however, where this can be varied. For example, where you are recruiting a PE teacher then a coaching session would be worthwhile. Also, if a music teacher were asked to take an orchestra practice, the data would be valuable to informing the recruitment process. This is a decision you should consider with care and be aware of how you might feel in the same situation.

2. Do you want the candidates to perform a task?

The intention that underpins both teaching a lesson and performing a task is twofold. First, it is to find a way of getting beyond the application form – to find out more about the person – and second, it is trying to validate the application form and the references. Is the person on the application form the person in front of us now?

There are tasks which can be set which facilitate this effectively and, used wisely, can provide a good basis for questions later on. In the next task you are asked to consider the kinds of tasks that candidates are set and to think about how they can be used to greatest effect.

TASK 28

Assessing candidates at interview

Table 6.3 lists a number of tasks given to candidates at interview.

Write down the criteria on which you would assess the task and the information this would give you, as the middle manager.

TABLE 6.3 The usefulness of interview tasks

Task	Assessment criteria	How this would inform the interview process
Presentation on a topic	■ Candidates' presentation skills ■	■ Candidates' confidence with an audience ■
Written answer to a question	■ Candidates' powers of expression	■ Candidates' ability to think on the spot ■
Observed discussion	■ Interaction with others ■	■ Interpersonal skills
Evaluation of a teaching resource	■ Relating knowledge to a teaching situation	■ How focused is the candidate on the job of teaching? ■ Open to change?

3. Do you intend to hold panel interviews only?

Panel interviews are where the candidates are interviewed by small groups of people, or alone. Typically, candidates will be interviewed by, for example, the middle manager (perhaps with a Governor), a member of the senior management team and others. The panels will come together and make a decision based on the candidate's performance in the interviews.

The advantages of this process are that, for people new to the profession, this can be less daunting than six or seven people firing questions at them. Also, people find it harder to sustain any deficiencies in their application if the process is extended over a period of time. This is not to suggest that candidates deliberately mislead those who interview, but it is necessary to acknowledge that when people want a job, they are capable of exaggeration and self-aggrandisement. The process which seeks to authenticate the application is called triangulation. This is where the application form is checked out via the references and the interview questions. The principle is that where a candidate makes an assertion in their application, this is tested out by looking at the reference and by the asking of a pertinent question.

The disadvantage of panel interviews is that there is less control over the interview process and there is less opportunity to see candidates answering questions on a range of topics. This illustrates the need for you to agree the process with the headteacher, so that the elements of the recruitment process are seen as complementary.

4. Will the process be by panel interviews followed by final interviews?

The advantage of following panel interviews with a final interview are that it addresses the deficiencies pointed out in the preceding section. The main disadvantage is time. A full recruitment process with tasks, panel interview and final interview will take up an entire day. However, this is time well spent if the end result is an appointment about which everyone is confident.

5. How will you inform candidates and what feedback will be offered to the unsuccessful?

Many teachers will recall being kept in a room until the successful candidate was offered the job and then being offered feedback. Schools have changed their procedures in that candidates can be telephoned in the evening with the news. There are a number of advantages to this:

- There is not the pressure to make a decision quickly (knowing that there are five or six people sitting outside as the clock ticks by can force the pace unnecessarily).

- The preferred candidate can be offered the post and if it is declined, the subsequent candidate need never know (we all like to think we were the first choice!)

- The candidates have had time to distance themselves from the school and so will accept with surety (the emotion of an interview day can lead people to make decisions they later regret).

- Feedback can be offered without the rawness of the interview process having being recently concluded.

- It seems less brutal and more humane.

Again, these decisions will need to be taken at a school level, but it is important to have a view on these matters and be able to exercise the judgement they bring to the recruitment of the teacher to the team.

Conducting an interview

Having decided the format for the recruitment process, the next matter to consider is how to conduct the interview itself. For the most part, newly appointed middle managers will have been on the receiving end of an interview process but being involved in the recruitment of a new team member for the first time can be quite daunting. The responsibility that goes with the decision-making process is understandable, but there are a number of pointers which can aid the task ahead.

By focusing on the person specification, the agenda for the interview starts to draw together. However, the purpose of the interview needs to be explored. In the main, the appointing panel will have a quantity of information about each candidate. The task is moving from information to a possible interview question. Table 6.4 below sets out how this can be achieved.

TABLE 6.4 Interview questions

Information and source	Areas for question in the interview	Issues which arise
Educational background of the candidate	<ul><li>What characterised your own schooling?</li><li>What memories do you have of your own schooling?</li><li>What features of your own education do you bring to your work as a teacher?</li></ul>	<ul><li>Is this person in teaching as a response to their own?</li><li>Is the candidate reflective?</li><li>Does the person look forward or back?</li></ul>
Subjects studied at school and University	<ul><li>Why did you choose to study…?</li><li>What were the best things about studying…?</li></ul>	<ul><li>Commitment to the subjects</li><li>Range of educational experience</li></ul>

Information and source	Areas for question in the interview	Issues which arise
	■ Would you recommend a course in...?	■ Ability to move from personal experience to advising students in school
Teaching practice (or previous experience for subsequent teaching posts)	■ Describe your first teaching practice/post? ■ What did you learn from this? ■ Describe an incident which challenged your view of education. ■ What is your teaching style? ■ What are the elements of a good lesson?	■ Does the person have significant experience? ■ Has the person learnt from their experience? ■ Does the person refer matters appropriately? ■ Does the person have a view on what constitutes effective teaching? How does this relate to their answers to questions on their own experience?
Extra-curricular involvement	■ What is your involvement in...? ■ What do you think is the place of extra-curricular activity? ■ Who should be involved? ■ How can we increase the involvement in extra-curricular activity?	■ What is the person's view of education as a holistic experience? ■ Does the person have ideas? ■ Is the person committed to the culture of the school?
References	■ Does the reference support the application?	■ Do the application, references and responses triangulate?

There are particular issues when appointing a newly qualified teacher (NQT) which need to be considered. These are to do with recruitment, interviewing and induction.

It is beneficial to establish relationships, where possible, with education departments in universities and colleges of further education. Where there is a vacancy in the school which would suit an NQT, the department can advise on suitable candidates. The advantage of this is that over time, colleges and schools can develop a mutually supportive relationship and students can be suitably appointed. There is clearly a cost benefit too. Some schools who have a large turnover will involve themselves in the Graduate Fairs at universities, but this is less common.

Newly-qualified teachers come to schools with enthusiasm and ideas, untainted by experience. The profile of NQTs has changed over the years to include people on their second careers. This can be as the result of lifestyle changes brought on by redundancy, return to work, etc. Thus, by seeking to appoint an NQT over a teacher with two or three years' experience, the team may not appoint the youngest person available. Our view is that appointment should not be on the basis of age alone – to do so would be discriminatory. The appointment process has to be fair and you have a responsibility to ensure that the processes set up will stand up to inspection.

Some colleges of education are proactive about preparing their students to make applications and provide them with opportunities to do mock interviews. However, there is no substitute for the real thing and it is important to be sensitive to the needs of these young (in professional terms, at least) people. A useful caveat when interviewing an NQT is to appoint on the basis of what they will be and what they have to offer, rather than what they are at this time.

The overall framework for the interview process has to be designed to see what people can do and what they might offer the team and the school. The time spent on this will be rewarded only if the assessment techniques are appropriate to the profile being sought.

TABLE 6.5 Summary of the recruitment process

To summarise, the recruitment process should:

- start with a team audit
- contain a person specification
- contain a job description
- advertise explicitly for the person required
- select on the basis of the person specification
- provide opportunities for the candidates to demonstrate what they can offer
- facilitate the triangulation process to authenticate the candidate's responses

_____ Recruiting a deputy subject leader _____

The process of recruiting a deputy subject leader is, in many respects, similar to that required when recruiting any other member of the team. However, because of the close professional working relationship between the subject leader and the deputy, there is a greater emphasis on the person specification and its relationship to the team audit.

Whilst the audit of skills and attributes will identify key characteristics which will need to be addressed in the recruitment process, it is important to appreciate that in recruiting a deputy subject leader, you are, potentially, recruiting your successor and to that end the National Standards for Subject Leaders can be a source of clarity in defining the role.

The core purpose of the subject leader is, according to the National Standards:

> 'To provide professional leadership and management for a subject to secure high quality teaching, effective use of resources and improved standards of learning and achievement for all pupils.'

To this end therefore, the deputy subject leader will need to be developed to take on this whole team role. However, if they are to do this then they need to provide evidence that they can do this (to some extent, at least) and have the ability to do this (in the future). Therefore, when analysing the applications for a deputy subject leader, you need to consider the job description more closely.

TASK 29

Defining the role of the deputy subject leader

Consider the range of tasks you would expect a deputy subject leader to undertake.

The principles which underlie each job description are that:

- the postholder should be responsible to you, as line manager
- there should be administrative tasks
- there should be developmental tasks
- there should be opportunities for the postholder to develop managerial and leadership skills
- the job description should mirror that of the team leader.

The acid test of a job description is that the postholder should know exactly what they have to do and to whom they have to report. It should be a document of clarity and definition. Whilst the contracting that is a necessary part of effective delegation is excluded from the job description, there is no doubt who is responsible for the delivery of the tasks set out.

To define a job description purely in administrative terms is poor because not only would it be very dull but it would not raise standards of teaching and learning. Also, setting out a job description which is entirely administrative gives the middle manager a heavy burden in monitoring the work that is being done. There needs to be some administrative input because:

1 It shares the load of administration across the team.

2 It frees the middle manager for other tasks.

3 It provides a range of experiences for the postholder to develop management skills.

The job description should be developmental in that it gives the postholder the opportunity to create and manage projects. Some projects can be far-reaching and wide-ranging depending on the type of school. A postholder who is, for example, Deputy Head of the junior school in a large Primary, might develop the personal, social and health education curriculum across the Key stage. This would clearly be a major project which would give the postholder the opportunity to develop significant skills in:

- project planning
- project management
- the change process
- monitoring the work of others
- preparing reports for the line manager, and many other opportunities.

Such a job description would enable the postholder to develop sufficient skills to be able to move to a middle management role of their own in time.

In some teams it is possible for the deputy to have a job description which mirrors that of the middle manager. This is usually possible only in larger schools where there are more tasks to be undertaken. An example of this is where the head of subject has overall responsibility for the subject but specific responsibility for Key Stage 4; the deputy subject leader's job description mirrors this by having responsibility for Key Stage 3.

The job description is not a tablet of stone. It represents a list of tasks to be undertaken for the period of time it covers. It is important because it sets out the agenda for what needs to be done.

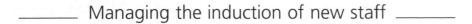

Managing the induction of new staff

Newly-appointed staff to any school or any post will, naturally, experience some anxiety as they prepare for their new job. As was remarked at the start of this chapter, teaching is unusual in that a change of job will normally be predicated by a change of school – all that is familiar is gone. You can do a great deal to facilitate the smooth induction of the new teacher. The following case study illustrates this.

CASE STUDY

Taking on an NQT (1)

Stephen is Head of Juniors at Leckie Primary School. The school has recently appointed Graham to the staff to teach a Year 5 class from September. Graham is an NQT. He interviewed very well but his references indicated that there were problems with lesson planning which were not fully resolved during teaching practice.

Stephen is preparing for the first induction meeting with Graham two weeks before the Summer term ends.

How should Stephen prepare for this interview?

In planning for this interview, Stephen needs to consider the following points:

1 Graham interviewed well and so there are qualities which he has which were able to override any concerns about lesson planning. He should make a list of these qualities and use these to strengthen Graham's work.

2 If the concerns about lesson planning are to be addressed, this needs to happen from Day 1. It is better to set up a monitoring process which supports Graham in the first few months than to wait for things to go awry. This is proactive management.

3 When preparing for the discussion on lesson planning with Graham, Stephen needs to decide if he will disclose the information from the references. He should take advice on this from the headteacher. As the reference is confidential to the headteacher, Stephen needs to be guarded. However, it is possible to raise these issues with Graham without referring to the reference received.

4 Stephen needs to clarify what he expects in terms of lesson plans and make this explicit to Graham during this interview. It would be advantageous to produce a proforma for Graham to use. By setting out the expectations he has clearly, there is no room for ambiguity. Stephen will need to guard against 'bamboozling' the new teacher, but the outcome should be that the new teacher feels supported in what he has to do.

5 There needs to be a programme which sets out how Graham will be inducted into the school – this will address any fears that he may have.

6 The date of the first meeting when Graham is in post will need to be set.

The benefit of this active meeting where the issues are set out and a process outlined is that it sets clear expectations and provides obvious support. It means that the new teacher is encouraged to work to high standards from Day 1. It may be that the fears are groundless – but few would argue that a planned induction to a new organisation is anything other than a good thing.

CASE STUDY

Taking on an NQT (2)

Stephen meets with Graham after Graham has spent two weeks in the school. Graham has been submitting his lesson plans, as required, and all seems to be well.

How should Stephen prepare for the meeting?

The question which the more experienced middle manager would ask is: How do you know that all seems to be well? What evidence is there? There is a need for some lesson observation in particular, and the next section discusses how this can be incorporated and developed as part of a whole school system using the Ofsted framework. This is an essential and fundamental part of the management of any organisation. The process has been characterised as a cycle (DfEE Standards and Effectiveness Unit Website November 1998).

Monitoring and evaluation

In the Chief Inspector's Report on the first cycle of inspections of schools (1998), monitoring and evaluation was found to be the most common area of weakness in school management. The existence of a structure for monitoring and evaluation which has procedures for assessing efficiency, effectiveness, equity and value for money, is considered essential if future decisions are to be based upon reliable data, but it appears that the processes of evaluation are often poorly understood. The extent to which evaluation does take place but essentially 'on the hoof' and in an unstructured way is demonstrated by the fact that of 117 [Ofsted] reports examined, only 54 per cent had some structured system...

The aim of monitoring and evaluating classroom practice is to raise the quality of the work of the school and hence raise achievement. In due course the procedure should move from simply monitoring of classroom practice into a biennial or even annual audit of all the work of the department, including analysis of the standards achieved by the students, the quality of education provided and leadership and management of the department. Monitoring and evaluation should progress into review and forward planning which takes place in the parallel system of team development planning.

Objectives

The long-term objectives for the planned system of monitoring and evaluation should be to:

1 Ensure that middle managers formally reflect upon practice in their departments.

2 Ensure that teaching staff have their lessons formally observed.

3 Consider whether pupils are achieving appropriate standards for their ability.

4 Provide an evidence base for forward planning.

5 Increase the middle manager's accountability for the work of their departments.

6 Improve the quality of management and leadership in departments.

The Ofsted framework provides a suitable basis to meet these objectives and, therefore, a system of monitoring and evaluation based upon it can be developed. This system provides an mechanism to monitor, evaluate and review the work of a team and also strengthens and improves the quality of middle managers.

In the early stages of lesson observations it is important to ensure that staff feel comfortable with being observed and having comments made about their work. In order to effect an improvement though it is necessary to move things to a more judgemental level where judgements are formed against agreed criteria. The Ofsted framework is the ideal vehicle for measurement and audit as it not only provides a comprehensive, thorough and rigorous set of standards against which judgements can be formed, it is also the instrument that will be used for testing the school.

Role of heads of departments

The National Standards for Subject Leaders include the explicit expectation that heads of departments should:

- ensure curriculum coverage, continuity and progression for all pupils
- use data to identify underachievement and make plans to rectify this
- provide guidance on appropriate teaching and learning methods as well as practices for assessing pupils' work
- evaluate the teaching of the subject
- establish clear expectation of staff involved with the subject
- audit training needs of staff
- ensure that the senior management team are well informed about subject policies, plans and priorities and success in meeting targets
- ensure the efficient deployment of resources.

In general terms the middle manager has the responsibility to bring this about and, therefore, needs evidence of teachers' work in order to facilitate this. It is advantageous to have an integrated system of monitoring, i.e. a process that monitors the work of the school across its breadth and depth. The Ofsted framework is an accepted standard by which schools are measured and therefore provides such a comprehensive approach. For the results of monitoring and evaluation to be acted upon in a cooperative way it is important that a wide range of staff have ownership of the process. It should not be seen as something that is 'done to them'. Associated with the previous point, the emphasis for evaluation and review must be placed upon the key people who have to act as a result in the case of classroom work in subjects this is the middle manager. This process successfully achieves this. In a successful department it is important that success is recognised by the monitoring process. The framework provides objective criteria against which achievement can be recognised. Where there are difficulties then the process must provide a supportive professional context in which to face up to those difficulties.

Fundamentally, this process is about management by objectives. It is about ensuring that teachers are all engaged on work which is consistent with the school's overall objectives as identified by the aims of the school. It is also, however, about participation in the process, better communication and enhanced motivation through clearly identified goals and the achievement of results.

In the previous chapter we discussed the appraisal and performance management structures. The appraisal interview is the one formal occasion in the year when the teacher and the line manager sit down to discuss work performances; but there needs to be an ongoing discussion, particularly if improvement needs guiding and monitoring.

The monitoring system must be consistent with the school culture. Fidler (1984) argues that if the organisation is participative, dynamic and has a clear sense of direction, then the appraisal and monitoring systems should reflect this by following a target-setting, problem-solving approach. There are issues particular to education that need to be discussed.

Handy (1995) describes many professionals as independent operators and in this model, management and appraisal are inappropriate. However, as organisations become more complex, coordination of some kind is required and for larger organisations some form of management is essential, particularly in turbulent times. With the gradual acceptance of management in education, a balance has to be struck between management approaches and professionalism.

Assessing the work of teachers is particularly difficult. There have been attempts to set down the criteria for good teaching (Ofsted, MacGilchrist et al. (1997)), but there are no universally agreed criteria. More fundamentally the relationship between teaching and learning is not direct. What has been set out here, however, is a realistic standard of performance.

TABLE 6.6 Summary of the monitoring process

The essential features of the monitoring systems are that it should:

- be part of the management process
- be positive and developmental whist still maintaining credibility as a check on quality
- ultimately improve the learning experiences of pupils and students.

Abridged from Fidler (1984)

———— Summary ————

Our intention is that, at the end of this chapter, you will have:

- considered the elements of a successful recruitment
- drawn up a person specification and a job description

- thought about the nature of motivation and how it affects your own work and that of others
- determined an induction process for new staff
- appreciated the need for lesson observation as part of the induction and monitoring process.

chapter seven

Making presentations

Planning the content

Deciding the form

Making an impact

Presentations to parents

Summary

G ood presentation skills are essential for influencing opinion and changing minds. The ability to stand in front of a group of people and present your views on a particular topic is a fundamental part of the role of most middle managers. Certainly when people are contemplating promoting someone to senior management, then it is likely that a presentation will be part of the selection process.

In this chapter, we are going to discuss the practical aspects of making a presentation. This will concentrate, in the main, on how to prepare materials for a presentation, but will also consider the ways in which the message can be put across in the most productive manner. Making presentations is a personal matter: it is about a personal style which the middle manager brings to the topic being discussed. However, there are particular skills and techniques that can be effective and transform the presentation being given.

Later in the chapter, we discuss the value of presentation in the context of subject and curriculum evenings. Many schools hold evenings for parents where teachers work alongside groups of parents on curriculum areas and more general topics such as homework. Middle managers are likely to be involved in these events; if they do not occur in school, you might wish to propose these as part of the school's development plan.

———— Planning the content ————

Creating an effective presentation starts with the remit. The first few questions to answer are:

1 What is the subject of the presentation?

2 How long does the presentation have to last?

3 Who is the audience for the presentation?

4 How does this presentation fit into the event as a whole?

These questions are important to answer at the early stage because they inform the entire planning stage.

First, what is the subject of the presentation? The talk may be on the subject of, for example, underachieving boys. If the task of doing the presentation has been given by the senior team, then you will need to negotiate the kind of presentation that is anticipated. However, more of this later.

Second, how long is the presentation to last? Planning a ten-minute presentation with, perhaps a plenary to follow is a different affair to the hour-long slot on a Homework evening. This will be important when deciding what you are going to say and how you will structure the presentation.

Third, who is the audience for the presentation? The people listening to your presentation can range from parents (with or without students), teachers (colleagues from and beyond your own school) and Governors. The type of audience that you will address will clearly have an impact on the type of presentation you plan.

Lastly, how does this presentation fit into the event as a whole? It is important, at the planning stage, to know what will happen before and after your presentation. It may be that there have been other presentations before yours. For example, an evening on GCSE Coursework might include presentations by a number of people including the Year Head, Subject leader for English, Subject leader for Mathematics, etc. By thinking through what has gone before, you can ensure that your presentation makes the point, but does not repeat either the message or the format of previous speakers.

There are a number of elements to successful presentations and the most fundamental is planning. Once you have decided the subject of the presentation, this task will help you to plan it.

TASK 30

Planning a presentation

You are to do a presentation to the staff at your school on the subject of 'Underachieving Boys'.

Brainstorm the ideas you would have on this subject.

List

- the main issues

- the opportunities for improvement

- practical tasks that can be undertaken

- the ways in which the programme can be monitored
- the ways in which the strategy can be evaluated and reviewed.

At this brainstorming stage, it is important to collect as many ideas as possible on the subject – you can edit the material later on and it is always easier to edit out than to add in.

The main issues for this presentation might be written in a 'mind-map' format (*see* Fig. 7.1).

FIG. 7.1 Mind-map of planning a presentation on underachieving boys

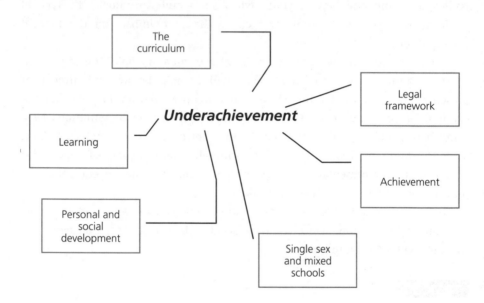

By breaking the subject into these topic headings it is then possible to consider the main issues in turn. The next stage is to plan around the subject headings and to think through the message that is being put forward.

In this case, the audience for this presentation is the staff and therefore you need to consider the issues as they affect the school.

It is always useful to start such a presentation with an overview of the topic; in this context you might wish to include:

■ performance data at a National level for different subjects

■ performance data at different levels (e.g. Key Stages, GCSE, A Level, etc.)

- changes in assessment criteria and syllabuses which might be relevant

- what the issues are for the school – how the school fits into the National pattern.

By opening the presentation in this way you can demonstrate an awareness of the National picture and, further, show the impact that this has on the school.

By taking each of the headings in turn and thinking through the issues as they affect the school, you will quickly build up a body of information which you can use for the presentation.

Deciding the form

At this stage it is worthwhile thinking through how the presentation is going to be made. The most popular form of presentation is the OHP or projector-based talk using transparencies or slides to pick out the salient points and then talking around them.

The advantage to this form of presentation is that it gives the audience something to look at whilst you talk. It can be difficult to sustain concentration over time and the bullet points which are included in the slides can be useful to make particular points clear. The disadvantage is that the business of producing the slides, or operating the projector can detract from the importance of the message. However, Microsoft's PowerPoint is useful when producing slides for use in a presentation.

The features that PowerPoint offers include:

- presentation formats which can be adapted easily

- colour presentation with pictures either from Clip-Art or other sources

- notes pages and handout masters – these are good for preparing the talk and handing out to those attending.

A presentation on the topic of 'underachieving boys' might look like this:

SLIDE 1

The talk begins with the title – this gives you the opportunity to introduce yourself to the audience and to set out the presentation. A picture brings the presentation to life. At this stage, you would set out the National data on underachievement and explain how the school fitted into this pattern. This will provide a context for the rest of the presentation. At this stage, you can state what the major issue is.

SLIDE 2

> It is truth universally acknowledged that a single boy in possession of a good brain, must be in want of an education.
>
> *abridged from Jane Austen's* Pride and Prejudice

By using a quotation, an audience of teachers will begin to engage in the subject matter. Such a tactic might be inappropriate for a more mixed group. Introducing the topic like this also opens the way to give a historical overview. You may choose to discuss the history of boys' education and how it has changed through time.

SLIDE 3

> Boy, Girl, Boy
>
> or
>
> *Girl, Girl, Girl*

Having just a few words on a slide is an effective device for making a particular point. The issue here is the fact that girls are outperforming boys and the impact this is having on post-school opportunities. The talk can broaden to include the idea that the system perhaps intrinsically favours girls.

SLIDE 4

> Write down the names of 5
> boys in a class you teach.

This slide is designed to introduce an element of interaction into the presentation. This can be very powerful and demonstrates to the audience that the issue is one that will affect them. However, by involving the audience, you have to respond to them; this requires a measure of confidence as it will inevitably involve dealing with a range of responses – in some cases responses may be cynical or uncooperative. The challenges may be considerable and they may introduce unwelcome comments; you need to plan the responses that you will make and ensure that the facts and figures to support any argument are readily available.

In addition, opening up the discussion can place constraints on the time allowed for the presentation. As such, this is a risky strategy; to curtail contributions can appear to stifle debate, but to permit too free a discussion might mean a presentation that over-runs.

SLIDE 5

> What are the issues for us?
>
> ■ boys are more likely to be excluded than girls
> ■ boys dominate lower sets
> ■ boys become less employable
> ■ boys lose their role models
> ■ boys don't work

The objective of this slide is to draw attention to the consequences of inaction and maintaining the status quo. By focusing attention on the results of the problems being posed, you are introducing a strategic overview.

SLIDE 6

> ## Why has this happened?
>
> - new ways of learning have improved girls' chances
> - new ways of working have improved women's prospects
> - social changes have made men less important in a family situation

As the presentation continues you are widening the discussion to look at the potential causes of the problem of underachievement. The previous slide exposed a number of symptoms and consequences. By outlining the possible reasons for the imbalance, you can demonstrate an awareness of the underlying causes and that you are in a position to articulate potential solutions. This is important because the world of education is full of people who are able to expose problems, but there is a need always to move the matter forward to the challenges and practical issues.

SLIDE 7

> ## How do boys begin?
>
> - computer games
> - play games which don't demand language
> - do things

The purpose of this slide is to start to unpick the problem and to put in place a number of ideas that can be developed into a set of proposals for action. The actual strategies that are set out in this presentation are less important than the point that, in setting out the argument, you are demonstrating an understanding of the issues and using a range of tactics to present the materials to the audience.

SLIDE 8

> ## How do girls begin?
>
> - encouraged to listen
> - play games demanding imagination
> - spend more time with adults

This slide is presented to create a contrast with the previous slide. Note that the format of the slide is identical – the key words are kept the same, with small changes that you can draw to the audience's attention.

SLIDE 9

> ## But what can we do?
>
> - types of work
> - classwork tasks
> - homework tasks
> - thinking
> - doing
> - reflecting
> - making them work
> - learning strategies
> - making boys think
> - making girls do

As the presentation starts to draw to a close, you can begin to set out the ways in which the issue can be addressed in school and the range of actions that can be taken. Having taken a historical perspective to explain why there is underachievement, you have produced evidence to support the assertions. By taking a wider perspective, you demonstrate a broad knowledge of the issues. By moving the presentation to a consideration of the practical matters involved in tackling the problem, the presentation sustains its impact.

SLIDE 10

DOING

- we can recognise that boys work differently from girls

- we can use strategies to help boys to think in different ways

- we can plan the work to optimise everyone's learning

Whilst the audience may enjoy listening to you speak, the purpose of the presentation is to set out a framework for the school to act. Completing the presentation with an overview of the strategies identified in the previous slide will enable you to move the audience forward.

Making an impact

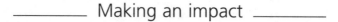

The use of colour and pictures can add tremendous impact to a presentation. This can be particularly so when dealing with a topic that may be unexciting. Also, by using bold colours or some of the fun pictures available from ClipArt or on the Web, it is possible to liven up any topic. Using colour and pictures also demonstrates a commitment to the audience. A well-presented talk with good quality slides shows a person in command of their work. This inspires confidence. It may be possible to include video or sound clips as part of a presentation. These have tremendous potential in any talk.

Microsoft PowerPoint software enables anyone charged with making a presentation to produce quality slides and handouts to match. The value of handouts is a judgement that you have to make, but the advantages are as follows.

- When handouts are distributed before the presentation begins, people do not feel the need to take notes as the slides are produced.

- The agenda for the talk is set out. This means that if anyone wishes to make a point, then they can see how you will address all the major issues in the talk.

- They help sustain the professional approach to the task.

- The production of these handouts helps to add weight to the importance of the talk; it demonstrates commitment to the task in hand.

There are a number of practical matters to consider when starting to prepare more fully for the presentation. These centre around what you intend to do and what you expect of your audience when they listen to your presentation.

It is important that your presentation makes an impact. Therefore, the script needs to be rehearsed sufficiently to ensure that it runs to time and that all the important points are made. It is better to deliver a short relevant presentation than a longer waffle. The script, the slides and the notes will help in this respect. To this end it is worthwhile timing the talk and using a stopwatch or some other device to keep to time when doing the presentation. Some OHPs have a clock at the front. A computer will have a clock on it. Otherwise, put a watch on the table where you can see it easily.

When setting up the venue it is important to think through where people will sit, where the projection device is placed and where you will stand. It is too easy to fall into the trap of standing in front of the projector and not realising this until later. Many people who are right handed find standing with the OHP on their right helps. In this way they will stand with their script in their left hand and place the slides on the OHP with their right. Typically people will turn in the direction of their dominant hand when speaking. This allows the presenter to act naturally. Also, standing side-on to the audience enables a more open style rather than the more confrontational face-on. However, this is a matter of preference. Some speakers prefer a lectern, which gives them somewhere to place their papers and somewhere to rest their hands.

Body language is very important to the overall effect of the presentation. Many people are nervous when giving their first few presentations. Practise open gestures – such as open hands and smiles – to avoid any potential difficulty. However, it is important to smile when it is natural.

There are a number of tips that are useful when thinking about delivering a presentation.

TABLE 7.1 Tips for effective delivery of a presentation

- Smile when it feels natural.
- Limit movement and stand straight – do not fidget with your hands.
- Do not maintain eye contact with one person for too long – it can be embarrassing.
- Gestures should be expansive and firm.
- Pause briefly before making major point.
- Do not leave visual aids on the screen for too long – they can be distracting.

- Watch for signs of boredom – fidgeting, yawns, looking around.
- Signpost key points throughout the presentation.
- Stick to time.

Many middle managers will have tales to tell about presentations they have delivered. The key for the novice presenter is to rehearse well and to concentrate on the delivery. It is worthwhile to seek feedback. In the same way as a teacher's skill develops through practice and feedback, the ability to deliver an effective presentation to a group of teachers is a skill that is acquired through time.

Presentations to parents

An increasingly important part of the middle manager's work is the organisation of subject evenings or other presentations to parents. Schools which are tackling issues such as homework, or informing parents about the Literacy strategy, for example, will consider a presentation to parents to tell them about the work that is to be done at school. The guidance for the presentation itself is the same, but there are important differences that need to be considered when planning.

First, the audience is usually a lay group. The jargon of teaching and education has become such a prevalent part of the way in which we talk that it is often difficult for us to appreciate how incomprehensible it is. The planning of such an evening will start with the brainstorm of ideas that need to be communicated. However, there a number of questions that you should ask when organising such an event.

TABLE 7.2 Planning a parent information event

- What is the purpose of the event? – Is it to give information? Is it to give guidance?
- Who is the sponsor for this event? Has the idea come from parents? The senior management team? Me?
- How does this event fit in with other events? – Is it part of a programme or is it the first time anything like this has been done?
- What is the anticipated response? Will there be a lot of parents who attend?
- How many other teachers will be there? Will they be subject specialists or the tutor team?

- Is there a budget for this event?

- How would you describe the parents group? Educationally aware? Interested?

There follows an example of a slide presentation prepared for a group of parents who wanted to know more about the National Curriculum and how they could help their children do better in Mathematics.

SLIDE 1

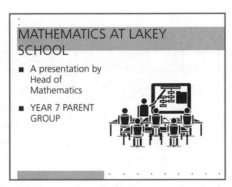

The purpose of this slide is to set out what the evening is about. This allows the middle manager (in this case the Head of Mathematics) to be introduced to the parents and to outline the format of the evening. In addition, the other attending teachers can be introduced. For the most part, the atmosphere needs to be relaxed and informal. The middle manager will be seen as the expert, but the opportunity to develop good relationships with the parents will be lost if the session turns into a lesson. Many middle managers will consider what they want to be called; do you want to introduce yourself as Mr Jones, or as Clive (or whatever)? The use of first names is an important consideration when setting the tone for such an event.

In addition, it will help if staff wear badges with their names and roles printed on. This will facilitate good relationships and help diffuse any awkwardness.

SLIDE 2

Agenda

- Mathematics and the National Curriculum
- Mathematics as a changing subject
- Key stages 3 and 4
- Activities
- Helping your child to succeed

This second slide sets out the agenda for the evening. The session begins with an explanation of the National Curriculum and sets out to define the words that teachers use, but many parents do not understand. It is very easy to presume that parents understand about Key Stages but their level of understanding is likely to vary considerably. However, providing that this is tackled in a sensitive manner, parents appreciate the gesture which seeks to explain, rather than presume.

SLIDE 3

Mathematics and the National Curriculum

- There are four areas of Mathematics:
    - MA1 – Using and Applying Mathematics
    - MA2 – Number and Algebra
    - MA3 – Shape and Space
    - MA4 – Handling data

This third slide is explaining in detail how the National Curriculum in Mathematics is structured. Clearly, a presentation on the Literacy Strategy would have similar headings which set out the different elements of the strategy. Although you might consider this kind of information redundant, it has the effect of engaging parents in the work that is being done. By 'de-bunking' the jargon – by explaining that 'shape' is about geometry – you are helping parents to understand the work that is being done.

SLIDE 4

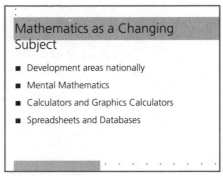

One of the comments frequently made to teachers – especially at Secondary school level – is that 'it's all changed'. An important outcome of an event such as this is to make parents feel that although much has changed, they can engage in their child's work. Furthermore, whilst much has changed, that reading is still reading, spelling is still spelling, and that by taking an informed interest in their child's education, they can support and improve their child's achievement.

If there is specialist equipment used in the delivery of the subject, showing parents how it is used will help to diffuse their fears.

SLIDE 5

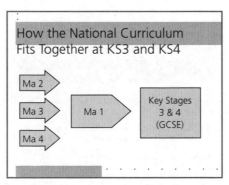

This slide is included so that parents can appreciate the nature of coursework and investigations. The purpose of such a slide is to inform parents about the work done at Key Stages 3 and 4.

In subjects where coursework is an important part of the assessment – and often a problematic aspect of a school's work – it is vital that parents understand how it fits in.

SLIDE 6

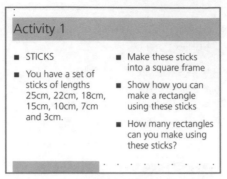

At this stage in the evening, it is beneficial to give the parents something to do. Whilst they have been sitting listening to the details of the National Curriculum, they may have been thinking about how this will affect them. Giving them an activity – working in groups is often a very good idea – helps to 'break the ice'.

Giving an activity which is practical and doesn't demand any subject knowledge is vital to the success of the evening. By organising an activity which encourages parents to talk to one another and gives the teachers the opportunity to join in helps to relax the groups. It would be possible to move this activity nearer to the start of the evening – this is a judgement you will have to make. However, by starting with a little talk allows people to relax a bit into the event.

SLIDE 7

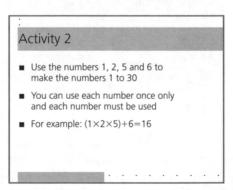

Having had a go at one activity, the event continues with a second, more challenging task. This kind of activity gets people talking about the subject and is sufficiently flexible to allow the presenter and the staff to join in. At this point, refreshments could be served – again to stress the informality of the event.

It is important that parents are not made to feel ignorant or foolish. This is a skilled task and requires the activities to be structured in such a way that everyone feels happy and understands how this relates to their child's work at school.

SLIDE 8

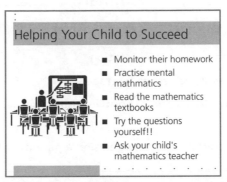

Helping Your Child to Succeed

- Monitor their homework
- Practise mental mathmatics
- Read the mathematics textbooks
- Try the questions yourself!!
- Ask your child's mathematics teacher

This last slide summarises the main points and draws the session to a close. It seeks to list the specific actions that parents can take to help their children with their Mathematics.

Planning a parents' subject evening or session is an effective way in which you can promote a subject or, as part of a whole school strategy, address a particular issue.

An important feature of such an event is the blend of formality and informality. When addressing issues with parents, you will want to consider the outcomes that are sought and plan the activities around these. Table 7.3 suggests a number of things that can be useful when planning these events:

TABLE 7.3 The practicalities of a parents' event

- Invite other teachers to join in the event – if it is a subject event, ask Heads of Year to join in.
- Engage the support of the management team, so that the event can be planned as part of a whole-school initiative.
- Provide badges for staff – decide on whether to use first names.
- Plan for refreshments.
- Plan activities that will enable people to work together and give staff the opportunity to talk to the parents.
- Decide on the seating – informal groups of tables are appropriate.
- Providing a handout at the end of the evening could be useful to parents.

Some people enjoy giving presentations – they enjoy the stimulus of preparing a talk and delivering it to a group of people. Others find it a difficult task. However, by looking for opportunities to present to an audience and not avoiding them you can develop the essential skills.

————— Summary —————

Our intention is that, at the end of this chapter, you will have:

- planned the content of a presentation
- reviewed a presentation stage by stage
- considered how to create a positive visual impact when making a presentation
- addressed the practicalities of organising a parents' information event.

chapter eight

Professional development

Management

Organisational theory

Teachers as learners

Summary

There has been a paradigm shift in the nature of school management and leadership over the past few years and it is with this in mind that we consider how to ensure that your career stays on track. Handy (1995) records how in the newer, more hi-tech organisations in the USA the word 'manager' had begun to disappear. People ceased to be described as 'managers'; they were identified as 'team leaders', 'project leaders', 'coordinators' or, more generally 'executives'. The language is significant because it signals a change in attitude and, perhaps, a new way of looking at the world. The implication behind the word 'manager' is that there are people to be managed and a stratified society.

Management

A further implication of this cultural shift is that management ceases to be a definition of status and becomes an activity. As such it can be defined and the associated skills taught, learnt and developed. Handy (1995) describes the position in the late 1980s as the 'hangover of management as a class' and the amateur status of British managers in comparison with managers in other countries. It is in this context that educational management needs to be seen. Educational management is, according to Glatter (1979) concerned with the 'internal operation of educational institutions, and also with their relationships with their environments'. School leaders play a key role in formulating the aims or goals of the institution. They have a particular responsibility for establishing and maintaining an effective management structure. These managerial functions might be regarded as essentially practical activities. Setting goals, making decisions and building relationships involve action. This, in part, explains the plethora of management courses which have been considered vital for any career teacher's professional development.

Some practitioners, however, have been dismissive of theories and concepts because they are thought to be remote from the realities of schools and classrooms. Bush (1989) describes a scenario where a manager takes a decision. In deciding on the most appropriate response to a particular problem the manager draws on a range of options suggested by previous encounters with this type of issue. If pressed to explain the reasons for the decision, the practitioner is likely to say that it is simply 'common sense'. However, this is based, often, on an implicit theory of the best way to deal with the situation. In a sense, theorising takes place without it being acknowledged as such. Bush argues, however, that those managers who operate on the basis of an unrecognised theory tend to have a one-dimensional outlook on organisational life simply as a consequence of being wedded to a single, narrow perspective.

This is not to argue that theory is more important than practice. Theory provides a rationale for decision making. It helps managers by giving them a basis for action. An appreciation of theory may also reduce the time required to achieve managerial effectiveness by compensating for a lack of certain levels of experience. This is how the middle manager moves from being a teacher to being an effective manager and leader.

Organisational theory

There has been a shift from management to leadership; there is also a sea change in the nature of organisational theory. It is necessary before considering the way in which successful schools operate to consider the bureaucratic model of school management articulated by Weber (1947). In a complicated article, Weber describes the nature of legal authority in an organisation. For Weber, a person in authority occupies an 'office'. In the actions associated with his/her status, including the commands he/she issues to others, the officeholder is subject to an impersonal order to which his/her actions are oriented. In this sense, the person who obeys authority does so is in his/her capacity as a member of the corporate group over whom the authority is exercised; his/her obedience is to the impersonal order.

It is worthwhile considering this model further. The organisation of these offices follows the principle of hierarchy, i.e. the lower office is under the control and supervision of the higher one. The rules which regulate the conduct of an office may be technical rules or norms. In both cases, if their application is to be fully rational, specialised training is necessary. Weber identifies particular features which are pertinent to this consideration of the school as an organisation:

- Teachers are organised in a clearly defined hierarchy of offices.

- Each office has a clearly defined sphere of competence, in the legal sense.

- Candidates are selected on the basis of technical qualifications. They are appointed.

- Teachers are remunerated by fixed salaries in money. The salary scales are primarily graded according to rank in the hierarchy; but in addition to this criterion, the responsibility of the position may be taken into account.

- It constitutes a career. Promotion is dependent on the judgement of superiors.

However, before we leave this analysis of the hierarchical model of school leadership it is useful to reflect on the ways in which schools in the twenty-first century still operate this paradigm.

TASK 31

Decision making

Consider the various jobs in schools and using Table 8.1 reflect on the ways in which they embody Weber's analysis of bureaucracy. You may want to add to the list some jobs we haven't mentioned and there is space for you to do so.

How are decisions made at your school?

Does this inform you on how to progress?

What is the impact of Threshold Assessment and the Leadership Group on this model?

TABLE 8.1 Decision making – Weber's model

Job title	What authority does the postholder have to make decisions?	How does this fit with Weber's model?
Head of Subject	■ Can purchase books and resources for the subject. ■ Develop the scheme of work for the subject. ■ 'The core purpose of the Subject Leader is to provide professional	■ Authority derives from the core purpose. ■ Purchasing authority is devolved within certain parameters. ■

Job title	What authority does the postholder have to make decisions?	How does this fit with Weber's model?
	leadership for a subject to secure high quality teaching, effective use of resources and improved standards of learning for all pupils' (*see* Chapter 2).	
Second in Department	■ ■ ■ ■	■
Year coordinator	■ ■ ■ ■	■
GNVQ coordination	■ ■	■
Senior teacher	■ ■ ■	■

The importance of this theoretical perspective lies in the framework that it gives to our understanding of how schools work as organisations. If you are to progress you need some understanding of the nature of a school as an organisation.

Weber provided the dominant theoretical perspective on organisations as bureaucracies. Despite the pervasive influence of Weber's work there have been few attempts to document applications of his theory to British education. One exception is the article by Harling (1984 in Bush, ed. (1989)) – this is useful further reading. The strength of this article lies in Harling's analysis of the complexity of

229

the educational system. The educational system as a whole is 'an organisation' and yet it possesses constituent 'organisations' at various levels. An organisation is one which exists and is formally established for the explicit purpose of achieving certain goals. In a bureaucracy, sub-units are clearly subordinate to the central leadership and are expected to accept, and work towards achieving, the goals set by the leaders. In a collegium it is assumed that members agree about the objectives of the institution because these are largely based on shared values. It depends on an initial agreement about aims. The notion of a collegial body as an educational institution derived from the essential difference between it and many other organisations, in that schools have large numbers of professional staff. Moreover, these professionals have substantial discretion in performing their teaching role. The effective management of schools depends on the cooperation of the professionals or, as a minimum, their acquiescence.

A key element to the collegial perspective is the professional competence of the teachers. In its purest form, all members of the collegium have an equal opportunity to influence policies. Noble and Pym (in Bush, ed. (1989)) discuss some of the difficulties that can arise when the collegial approach is accompanied by an elaborate system of committees. The adoption of collegial approaches has been particularly evident in primary schools where teachers are assumed to have a responsibility for one element of the curriculum as well as for teaching their own class.

An understanding of these issues is necessary before you can focus your attention on the moves you intend to make.

TASK 32

Decision making at your school

Think about your own school or the school you would like to work at and consider these questions.

At what level are the aims of the school decided and how are they decided?

How are decisions made at the school?

How would you describe the organisational structure?

Are there links between the school and the external environment?

How would you describe the leadership of the school?

In response to these questions, Table 8.2 compares the two organisational perspectives:

TABLE 8.2 Comparing organisational perspectives

Question	Bureaucratic perspective	Collegial perspective
At what level are the aims of the school decided and how are they decided?	Aims are determined by the headteacher and perhaps the senior management team.	There are policy groups which consider questions and create shared objectives.
How are decisions made at the school?	Decisions are based on objectives. There is an analysis of issues and decisions are taken in line with the hierarchical structure.	Decisions are characterised by thorough discussion proposals and collaboration.
How would you describe the organisational structure?	Decisions move from top to bottom. There are rigid job descriptions which are expressed in terms of production, evaluation, checking, reporting, etc. There is a sense in which collaboration develops from the structure.	Areas may be specified but are often negotiated and draw on strengths and expertise. The structure develops from the collaboration.
Are there links between the school and the external environment?	Parents will go through an established procedure. The headteacher reports to the Governors.	Links with other schools are created and sustained through networks. Typically each teacher has their own authority to contact parents.
How would you describe the leadership of the school?	This is characterised by: didactic rigid consultative deterministic leadership management.	This is characterised by: cooperation empathy discursive management.

The value in considering these perspectives (and other models explained in Chapter 4 – *see* page 113) is that they give us useful and valid insights into the nature of management. They represent different ways of analysing educational institutions. The applicability of each model depends on the nature of the organisation, the event or situation under consideration.

In recent years there has been a movement towards a fuller consideration of the nature of school leadership and from this has developed a concept whereby teachers and students became integrated into the process of leading a school. From this has emerged two fundamental processes: the exercise of leadership and the practice of teaching and learning. For years, those running the system: headteachers, teachers and school governors, knew nothing of research into school effectiveness and school improvement.

Brighouse and Woods (1989) describe the seven processes which encompass most activities in school life:

TABLE 8.3 Brighouse and Woods' seven processes

- the practice of teaching and learning

- the exercise of leadership

- the practice of management and organisation

- the practice of collective review

- the creation of an environment most suitable for learning

- the promotion of staff development

- the encouragement of parental and community involvement.

Teachers as learners

Improving schools are learning organisations – this theme has been discussed several times in this book. Teachers teach, but they also need to be advanced learners in order to develop new skills and insights. Teachers need to keep up to date with their area of expertise and with recent research about pedagogy. They have to keep up to date with legislative changes that affect their work such as the national curriculum, assessment, inspection and appraisal. Learning needs to be continuous in order to enable teachers to improve classroom practice, contribute to whole-school issues, manage change and acquire new skills.

MacGilchrist, Myers and Reed (1997) discuss motivation in teacher learning. There have been surveys of teacher morale; the long-term effect of being told that what is done is inadequate and references to the numbers of incompetent teachers are not conducive to high levels of morale. However, the literature on school improvement (reviewed in MacGilchrist et al.) suggests that teachers need to find both meaning and 'ownership' in order to want to participate in change efforts. As the future leaders of schools – whether at middle or senior level – teachers need to acknowledge the ways in which they can motivate their colleagues most effectively. As a leader, a teacher can be the one who provides the opportunities for learning to be put to good use and for the means of maximising student progress and achievement.

In seeking to make the transition from middle manager to senior manager, the teacher needs to consider the range of experiences that will be necessary for such a role.

The most important feature in a teacher's portfolio of experiences is that of excellence in the classroom and a record, over time, of successful teaching. To this end it is essential to keep records of the classes taught and the results obtained. This, of course, is required for threshold assessment.

The move to a more senior role is characterised by the nature of the job itself. As a senior manager, the responsibility lies not with a team of staff (e.g. a subject team, a year team, etc.) but with whole-school issues. The middle manager needs to get experience of involvement in and the leadership of initiatives to address whole-school issues. Further there are a range of tasks which are typically associated with senior management of which the middle manager can gain some experience. Table 8.4 sets out some of these tasks and identifies ways in which a teacher can become involved:

TABLE 8.4 Gaining involvement in senior management tasks

Senior management task	Involvement
Timetabling and curriculum planning	■ Join the timetable construction group or ask the teacher responsible if you can help. ■ Join the working party on curriculum planning. ■ Take responsibility for the organisation of student options (at Key Stage 4 or Sixth Form). ■ Lead a working party on marking policy, etc.
Organisation of major events and administration	■ Organise a school trip. ■ Produce a play. ■ Organise activity weeks. ■ Organise cover for exam week. ■ Organise the Key Stage tests.

Senior management task	Involvement
Working with Governors	■ Advise a Governors' committee. ■ Be a Teacher-Governor. ■ Be a Governor of another school.
Staff INSET	■ Lead staff INSET. ■ Join or facilitate a staff INSET working group.

Motivation to carry on is a complicated business. For some it will be the prospect of fame, power, money and success. For many people, however, it is the opportunity to create life chances for children that motivates them to continue. By continually focusing on that which improves the lot of children – at whatever phase of education we work in – we make sure that all that we do adds to the richness of school life. If you want to move beyond the role of middle manager this is addressed in the next book in the series.

 Summary

Our intention is that, at the end of this chapter, you will have:

■ considered management as a skill-based activity

■ thought about leadership in the context of school management

■ considered teaching as a learning-based profession

■ planned your own involvement in whole-school activities as part of a career plan.

References

Applebee, A. (1989) The Enterprise We Are Part of: Learning to Teach, *Developments in Learning and Assessment,* Eds. Murphy, P. and Moon, B., London: Hodder and Stoughton.

Bennett, N. (1987) Processes in the Post-Plowden Era, *Developments in Learning and Assessment,* Eds. Murphy, P. and Moon, B., London: Hodder and Stoughton.

Bennett, N. (1995) Introduction, *E828 Educational Management in Action* – Open University Study Guide, Milton Keynes: Open University Press.

Bowring-Carr, C. and West-Burnham, J. (1997) *Effective Learning in Schools,* London: Pearson Education.

Brighouse, T. and Woods, D. (1989) *How to Improve your School,* London: Routledge.

Bush, T. (1989) The Nature of Theory in Educational Management, *Managing Education: Theory and Practice*, Ed. Bush, T. (1992), Buckingham: Open University Press.

Campbell, J. (1989) The Education Reform Act 1988: Some Implications for Curriculum Decision Making in Primary Schools, *Approaches to Curriculum Management*, Ed. Preedy, M. (1992), Milton Keynes: The Open University Press.

Cohen, L. and Manion, L. (1977) *A Guide to Teaching Practice*, London: Methuen.

Combs, A. (1965) The Professional Education of Teachers, *A Guide to Teaching Practice* by Cohen, L. and Manion, L. (1977), London: Methuen.

Fidler, B. (1984) Leadership in Post-Compulsory Education, Ed. Harling, P. *New Directions in Educational Leadership*, London: Falmer Press.

Furukawa, H. (1982) Motivation to Work, *Human Resource Management in Education,* Eds. Riches, C. and Morgan, C. (1992), Buckingham: Open University Press.

Garland, H. (1984) Relation of Effort–Performance Expectancy to Performance in Goal-Setting Experiments, *Journal of Applied Psychology*, **69**.

Gibbons, M. (1977) Beyond the Sabre-Toothed Curriculum, *Approaches to Curriculum Management,* Ed. Preedy, M. (1992), Milton Keynes: The Open University Press.

Glatter, R. (1979) The Nature of Theory in Educational Management, *Managing Education: Theory and Practice,* Ed. Bush, T. (1992), Buckingham: Open University Press.

Gold, R. and Szemerenyi, S. (1997) *Running a School 1988: Legal Duties and Responsibilities*, Bristol: Jordans.

'Handbook of Suggestions for Teachers' (1959), *E819 Curriculum, Learning and Assessment* – Open University Study Guide (1995), Eds. Lawn, M., Moon, B. and Murphy, P., Milton Keynes: Open University Press.

Handy, C. (1995) *The Age of Unreason*, London: Arrow Books Ltd.

Harling, P. (1984) The Organizational Framework for Educational Leadership, *Managing Education: Theory and Practice*, Ed. Bush, T. (1992), Buckingham: Open University Press.

Heward, C. (1984) Parents, Sons and their Careers: A Case Study of a Public School 1930–50, *British Public Schools: Policy and Practice*, Ed. Walford, G. (1984), London: Falmer Press.

Jackson, S.E. and Zedeck, S. (1982) Explaining Performance Variability: Contributions to Goal Setting, Task Characteristics and Evaluative Contexts, *Journal of Applied Psychology*, **67**.

MacGilchrist, B., Myers, K. and Reed, J. (1997) *The Intelligent School*, London: Paul Chapman Publishing Ltd.

Perkin, H. (1969) The Origins of Modern English Society 1780–1880, London: Routledge and Kegan Paul.

'Primary Education' (1959) *E819 Curriculum, Learning and Assessment* – Open University Study Guide (1995), Eds. Lawn, M., Moon, B. and Murphy, P., Milton Keynes: Open University Press.

Pring, R. (2000) 'Educational Research: Working Together', Continuing Professional Development Conference, March 2000, University of Oxford Conference Notes.

Roberts, W. (1989) *Leadership Secrets of Attila the Hun*, London: Bantam.

Skilbeck, M. (1989) A Changing Social and Educational Context, *Policies for the Curriculum*, Eds. Moon, B., Murphy, P. and Raynor, J., Open University, London: Hodder and Stoughton.

Teacher Training Agency (1998) *National Standards for Subject Leaders*.

Weber, M. (1947) Legal Authority in a Bureaucracy, *Managing Education: Theory and Practice*, Ed. Bush, T. (1992), Buckingham: Open University Press.

Index

Applebee   4

Application process   22, 41–47, 53, 54,
   58, 192

Appointments
   Starting out   66–68, 86

Appraisal   149–155

Bennett   5

Bowring-Carr and West-Burnham
   9, 12

Brighouse and Woods   232

Bush   109

Campbell   184

Children's development   111

Cohen and Manion   7

Combs   8

Contracting   17–19

Culture of a school   88–90

Curriculum vitae   58

Delegating   19

Differentiation   12–17

Development plans   127–134

Fidler   205

Frustration   40

Furukawa   186

Garland   184

Gibbons   93

Glatter   226

Gold and Szemerenyi   150, 190

Handy   205, 226

Harling   229

Heward   138

Information about a school   41–49

Interview
   Assessment of candidates   192–198
   Etiquette   59
   Preparation   59
   Questions   61

Jackson and Zedeck   184

Job description   23, 51–53, 190

Learning
   and children's development   111
   as a process   8
   at the centre of the organisation   8
   styles of   12
   topic analysis   13–14

Letters for applications   53, 58

Line management
   and monitoring   139–141

Line management *continued*
  analytical and functional
    monitoring   142–145
  and being managed   148

MacGilchrist, Myers and Reed   8, 205, 232
Meetings
  initial team meetings   69, 72–74
  with the headteacher   69
Middle manager as
  an administrator   126, 163
  a change agent   88
  a class teacher   139
  and change models   92–98
  core purpose of   28
  a leader   104–109
  a leader of change   90–92, 127–134
  a life-long learner   20
  modern subject leader   31
  a person   86–87
  a professional   33–36
  a project leader   17
  a record keeper   164
  a visionary   115
  a life-long learner   20
Monitoring, characteristics of effective
    148
Motivation   37, 183–186

National Standards for Subject Leaders
    24, 29, 199, 204
Noble and Pym   230

Ofsted   2, 10–11, 119
Opportunity   40

Performance management   159–163
  linking to development planning
    161–163
  monitoring and review   162–163
Perkins   138
Person specification   49, 189
Presentations   60, 208–224
Professional development
  career development   20–22, 33,
    228–234
  management theory   226
  through research   5
Professionalism   32–33
Pring   5

Roberts   104

Skilbeck   7
Subject knowledge   3

Teaching
  excellence   2
  feedback on   83
  good teacher   6–9
  observation   9, 82–83
  scholarship   4
  subject specific knowledge   4
Team
  agenda   86
  deputy subject leader   199
  getting to know them   76–79, 85
  meetings   69, 72–76, 125–126
  needs   118–119
  NQT   201
  profile   80–81, 187–188
  recruitment   187
  reports   165–179

Team *continued*

  response to strategic change
      122–125

  strengths 120

  of teachers 82

  tackling difficult issues 155–157

  target setting 157

  of teachers 82

Time management 98–102

Weber 227